Bleeding Hearts

Bleeding Hearts

From Passionate Activism to Violent Insurgency in Egypt

Abdallah Hendawy

LEXINGTON BOOKS
Lanham • Boulder • New York • London

Published by Lexington Books
An imprint of The Rowman & Littlefield Publishing Group, Inc.
4501 Forbes Boulevard, Suite 200, Lanham, Maryland 20706
www.rowman.com

86-90 Paul Street, London EC2A 4NE

British Library Cataloguing in Publication Information Available

Library of Congress Cataloging-in-Publication Data

Names: Hendawy, Abdallah, author.
Title: Bleeding hearts : from passionate activism to violent insurgency in
    Egypt / Abdallah Hendawy.
Description: Lanham, Maryland : Lexington Books, 2021. | Includes
    bibliographical references and index. | Summary: "This book explores the
    wave of violent radicalization in post-2011 Egypt and argues that it is
    the result of unrelenting tension between aspirations, grievances,
    emotions, meanings, and societal beliefs. [The author] examines the wave
    of violence that broke out in Egypt in the aftermath of the 2013
    military takeover against the country's first democratically elected
    president. Abdallah Hendawy sheds light on stories of several political
    activists who abandoned their commitment to nonviolence and took up arms
    against the state. Through multiple interviews, ethnographic
    observations, field work, and qualitative data analysis, Hendawy
    challenges the dominant theoretical paradigms on radicalization that
    often attribute this complex phenomenon to ideological or religious
    beliefs. Hendawy thoroughly examines the tumultuous events that followed
    the 2013 military takeover and the journey of several radicalized
    individuals. He demonstrates how and why select Egyptian activists
    turned to violent tactics in the course of their political
    engagement."—Provided by publisher.
Identifiers: LCCN 2021038979 (print) | LCCN 2021038980 (ebook) | ISBN
    9781793613042 (cloth) | ISBN 9781793613059 (ebook) |
    ISBN 9781793613066 (pbk)
Subjects: LCSH: Political violence—Egypt—History—21st century. |
    Insurgency—Egypt—History—21st century. |
    Radicalism—Egypt—History—21st century. | Egypt—History—2011-
Classification: LCC HN786.Z9 V545 2021 (print) | LCC HN786.Z9 (ebook) |
    DDC 303.60962—dc2 3
LC record available at https://lccn.loc.gov/2021038979
LC ebook record available at https://lccn.loc.gov/2021038980

To the four most important women in my life:
my wife, daughter, mother, and sister.

Contents

Figures and Tables

FIGURES

TABLES

Timeline of Major Events

January 25, 2011	First rally rolls down the street demanding the removal of Egyptian President Hosni Mubarak.
January 28, 2011	Collapse of police forces and deployment of military forces nationwide to maintain law and order.
February 11, 2011	President Mubarak steps down and delegates his power to Supreme Council of Armed Forces (SCAF) to govern the country during the transition period.
March 19, 2011	Egyptians vote on a temporary constitutional declaration.
June 18, 2012	The Muslim Brotherhood's Mohammed Morsi wins the presidential election runoff with 51.7 percent of the vote and became Egypt's first freely elected civilian president.
December 22, 2012	Egyptians voted to approve a new constitution that was drafted by predominantly Islamist leaders.
June 30, 2013	Anti-Mohamed Morsi protesters take to the street demanding his removal.
July 3, 2013	Military intervenes, removing the elected president and appointing Egypt's Chief Justice Adly Mansour as an interim president, sparking clashes nationwide between pro- Morsi protesters and pro-military supporters.
August 14, 2013	Military and police forces use deadly force to clear pro Morsi stronghold Rab'a square sit-in.
October 9, 2013	The U.S. government suspends its military aid to Egypt citing state violence against anti-military coup protesters.

May 2014   Egyptian presidential election
June 30, 2014   Former defense minister Abdel Fattah El Sisi, assumes
                    office after winning 97 percent of the votes.

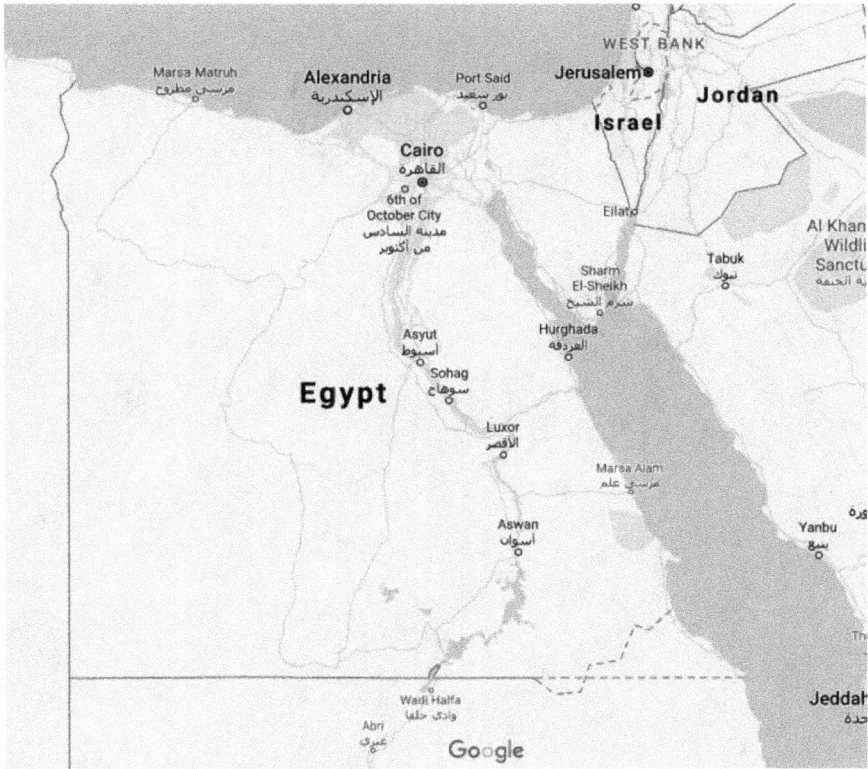

Map of Egypt Copyright: Google Maps

Preface

Egypt is home to ancient history, mythology, and a global field of study. It's over five-thousand years old and has produced some of the greatest advances in the history of the human race. Egypt is also my home. I was born and raised in Alexandria, walking distance from the Mediterranean Sea. It's where my family has lived as far back as we can trace. When I think of home, I think of the salty air on the Corniche (walkway by the sea), the fresh mango juice and sugar cane that I would grab on my walks home from school, the old architecture, the honking and constant noise, the thrill of football (soccer) matches, and the warmth of the people. I love this country, but—like the history of the country itself—it's complicated.

My generation has seen the rise and demise of a revolution, a brief era of democratic reform, and the reinstatement of a military dictatorship—with all that it entails. This book is not about my personal experience, although my direct engagement in activism and my strong nonviolent, pro-democracy views inform my perspective. This book is about a few young men who broke from their nonviolent commitments to carry up arms and target state officials. At the beginning of their stories, these men are like any of us—working hard, providing for their families, hopeful for their futures, and just trying to get by. Their struggles are relatable to a point, but there's a turning point in each experience where the common narratives stop and the move toward violence begins. This book explores that turning point and the impetus for this change: What happened that shattered their commitment to nonviolence? Why did they take up arms and decide that was the best pathway forward?

This book posits that violent insurgency is not merely the result of an interest in or pursuit of martyrdom (a commonly suggested answer); rather, violent insurgency is a strategic and tactical endeavor that is often justified by an individual (to themselves, as well as a claim made to others) after suffering a perceived injustice at the hands of an enemy. From the cases I examined, framing violent radicalization as an act of ideological or religious conviction provides a sort of cover story, a home that places the act within the narrative of a broader story and offers a convenient explanation to gloss over what is actually the far more complex phenomenon of violent radicalization. This is the focus of *Bleeding Hearts*.

Acknowledgments

This book is a result of several years of research and hard work. But this work would not have been possible without the help and support I received from key people throughout the process from the very early days up until the finish line. I would like to express my heartfelt gratitude and appreciation to everyone who helped me accomplish this work, either by guidance, advisory, review, criticism, or even moral support. But nobody has been more important to me in the pursuit of this project than my wife. She is my ultimate cheerleader, and the reason that motivated me every single day. For that, and for many other reasons, I thank her from the bottom of my heart.

Introduction

January 25, 2011 is a date that many young Egyptians of my generation will never forget. It is the day we saw the beginnings of an unprecedented pro-democracy movement that would, within eighteen days, topple one of the most rigid and long-standing dictatorships in the Middle East. Hosni Mubarak had been president of Egypt for more than thirty years. Since my birth until 2011 (twenty-four years old), I didn't know any other president to Egypt. His era was characterized with a bevy of tyrannical state practices and police brutality. After thirty years of resistance efforts, activists chose January 25—the National Police Day—as the appropriate symbolic day to protest police brutality and to demand the ouster of the Minister of Interior (Egypt's national chief of police). The marches took place throughout Egypt and the groundswell of support for this targeted initiative would, within three days, spark a nationwide uprising with much larger goals.

Toppling a long-standing despot whose era was famed with systematic abuses, human rights' violations, corruption, bad governance, and an assortment of authoritarian practices, was a remarkable victory for the pro-democracy movement in Egypt and would send waves of hope across the region. But this sudden ouster of President Mubarak represented just one drop in an ocean of changes that reached beyond the discernible political ramifications.

Over the two years following the fall of Mubarak (2011–2013), the country held its first free elections, wrote a new constitution, elected its first civilian president, and witnessed some monumental political and social adjustments to meet the new environment. As a participant of the uprising myself, I still recall every moment of it. From the throbbing fear of police confrontations in public squares, to the adrenaline rush that pairs every protest, all the way to the indescribable feeling of triumph when Mubarak stepped down.

It was the first time I, and many of the youth in Egypt, ever felt as though we had any influence over a political decision in this country. For the first time in decades, everyone in Egypt was talking about politics—freely and without the fear of arbitrary arrest, torture, and forced disappearance. Issues of governance, liberties, national identity, religion, constitution, and others were topics of daily discussion throughout Egypt.

From late 2011 through mid-2013, during the incompetent and polarizing, yet brief, governance of the Muslim Brotherhood, one could still see these political disputes and disagreements as part of the bourgeoning political process that would evolve and mature with time rather than indicators of a failed revolution.

But the euphoria didn't last long, and the gains made by the uprising were short-lived. In 2013, the nascent democracy movement was crushed. All reform efforts were upturned when the military generals swiftly seized power, removing the newly elected civilian President Mohamed Morsi, and instating one of their own after a sham election—which Abdel Fattah El Sisi won with a landslide victory.

The military generals accused the Muslim Brotherhood leaders of being conspirators and pushing the country to the edge of collapse which, the military claimed, necessitated the military coup d'état—"under popular demand"—to save the country. Such a move by the military sparked nationwide confrontations and led to the arrest, killing, and the detention of many pro-Muslim Brotherhood members but also many other activists who questioned the military's intentions or actions.

The roller-coaster trajectory of Egypt's pro-democracy movement from 2011 to the present day has impacted every segment of society—the political process and democratization efforts, to individual activists and advocates who participated in the movement. Activists have been arrested and thrown in jail on false charges, killed in confrontations with police or in mysterious circumstances, or simply disappeared with no trace—creating a rapidly deteriorating political climate that is arguably worse than Mubarak's era.

Amid the raging political turmoil, there was a conspicuous increase of violent insurgency in Egypt in mid- and late-2013 that materialized in different attacks targeting primarily police and military facilities, as well as state officials. And while the interim government—appointed by the military generals—principally blamed Muslim Brotherhood members, these accusations were often made without any known investigation or transparent examination to support them. In some instances, the blame was placed even before the attacks began (see Abdel Fattah El Sisi's speech in late July 2013).

The magnitude and frequency of the attacks increased over time. The government continued to assign blame to the Muslim Brotherhood as the principal perpetrator of all violent activities, ultimately classifying the organization as a terrorist group. Meanwhile, military loyalist pundits (media personalities) expanded on this narrative to frame the Muslim Brotherhood organization and its members as violent radicals and burgeoning terrorists.

While the Muslim Brotherhood has indeed had a history of violence—including after 2013—there is more to the story. Pundits and the military regime focused on one aspect of truth and failed to account for other variables—either intentionally or unintentionally—that were contributing to the sudden spike in violence.

I argue that this wave of violent radicalization in Egypt is the result of a culmination of events and experiences, the outcome of an unrelenting tension between aspirations, grievances, individual emotions, meanings, and societal beliefs. This unique combination of factors, in the context of post-revolutionary Egypt, is what I explore in this book.

In order to examine the unique intersection of these many different factors, we turn to the field of sociology. As the study of human social interactions, sociology lends us helpful theoretical and methodological approaches that we can use to answer the key questions that will help us understand what exactly happened in Egypt between the period of 2013 and 2020 (and perhaps in the future) that prompted a spike in violent insurgency among nonviolent activists.

The key questions are: if the protesters of the Egyptian revolution in 2011 managed to bring down a dictator and elect a new president using only nonviolent means, and were on the course to building their aspired democracy, why did some activists switch to using violent tactics in 2013? More importantly, why did the majority of the attacks target only government entities—namely the police and military? Put simply, what prompted this transformation from peaceful activism to violent insurgency?

Chapter One

Profound Trauma and
the Birth of Grievances

5:55 PM, JULY 14TH, 2014

**BREAKING NEWS: TWENTY-TWO PEOPLE KILLED AT
FARAFRA MILITARY CHECKPOINT
IN THE WESTERN DESERT OF EGYPT**

As details continued to roll in, analysts speculated that the attack had been carried out by one of the anti-government insurgent organizations (Yousef and El Bahrawy 2014). Eyewitnesses estimated there were ten to fifteen assailants. Masked men had initiated the assault by overwhelming the checkpoint with multiple RPG-7 grenades targeting the ammunitions depot causing instant explosions and massive fireballs. An exchange of fire broke out between the soldiers and the unknown assailants before the soldiers ran out of ammo and received reinforcements from the nearest military base. The assailants then retreated while shooting, ultimately leaving behind twenty-two dead bodies and four wounded in critical conditions.

July 14, the day of the attack, also marked the seventeenth day of Ramadan, the holiest month in the Islamic calendar. It is a month where Muslims from all around the world fast from sunrise to sunset. They abstain from eating, drinking, smoking, and more importantly, commit no sins whatsoever. Whether a faithful practicing Muslim or an occasional worshipper, Muslims pay a special reverence to this holy month.

The month's rituals go beyond the religious practices. Every Muslim country observes the month with a set of special traditions and celebrations in a form of special food, songs, and clothes. Egypt is well-known throughout the Muslim world for having very unique celebratory ambiance during Ramadan.

5

Children decorate alleyways, families gather for nightly iftars (the breaking of the fast), new seasonal holiday TV shows are produced, special meals are prepared and dispensed for free to the poor, among many other traditions. These celebrations are so pervasive in Egypt, that even non-Muslims get to share these traditions in their own way or together with their Muslim friends and neighbors as the religious holiday melds with the broader culture.

When the attack took place, it was shortly before the sunset—which is the iftar (breaking the fast) time. Meaning that the soldiers had likely been fasting since sunrise and were presumably preparing to break their fast or do their Maghreb (sunset) prayers. Sameh, a conscript who was deployed in a nearby base between 2013 and 2014 explained that Ramadan is a month when soldiers and officers enjoy more flexibility in their service hours and required duties. Standing military protocol technically requires that conscripts and officers are not supposed to leave their posts or gather for iftar, instead re-ceiving their meal at their service locations, whether on watch towers, gates, patrol passages, or elsewhere. However, due to the celebratory atmosphere of Ramadan, many of these protocols are loosely enforced and the environ-ment is generally laxer. "The minutes leading to iftar time are the toughest, everyone is tired, exhausted, and thirsty—especially in desert heat that could average well above 100F (37 C) during summertime," said Sameh.

The timing and magnitude of this attack—particularly during a high holy month dedicated to sanctity and goodwill—had a significant reverberating impact through Egypt. This was a uniformly devastating attack for Egyptians, regardless of political preference or party allegiance. Even among those critical of the military role in politics, the use of violence in such a manner, at such a vulnerable time, was publicly denounced. Reactions varied from questioning the motivation for and cause of the attack, while others prayed to the fallen soldiers and demanded retribution.

This July 14 attack was a pinnacle event—demonstrating the brutality that was surging as disenfranchised groups lashed out against the controlling forces—but it was also one attack of many. Violent events were on the rise throughout Egypt and the Egyptian government was facing mounting national and international pressure to explain it because these attacks did not appear to be random. These violent attacks targeted, almost exclusively, state institu-tions, namely military, police, as well as senior officials. According to several data points from the Global Terrorism Database, the spike of anti-government attacks begun in the months that followed the military coup d'état which was led by the then Minister of Defense Abdel Fattah El Sisi against the first democratically elected civilian president, Mohamed Morsi in July 2013.

A few weeks after the military coup took place, the Egyptian military de-clared its own "war on potential terrorism." In his speech on July 23, the then minster of defense, Abdel Fattah El Sisi, asked the Egyptian people to take to the street and show support to his campaign against what he called "potential terrorism." There were no clear details, information, or specifics on what was meant by "potential terrorism" either in legal or political terms.

This nebulous campaign opened the door for the government to accuse many groups of "terrorism" without any legal grounds or rational basis. Muslim Brotherhood, Al-Qaeda, Islamic State, together with other political groups—including liberal and leftist crowds and individuals—all were treated equally as "terrorists" and "outlaws."

The term "war on terror" was used arbitrarily to describe any political opposition group that posed a perceived threat to the military generals—the *de facto* rulers of the country following the removal of the elected president.

Less than a month after this tragic incident, another attack took place on another military check point. This time in the northern coast of Egypt at the Al-Dab'aa checkpoint, killing one military officer and four conscripts (El Badry et al. 2014). This was the officer's first day of work in this assignment. He was barely settling in his new job together with conscripts he had just met, when his life was taken away by a group of insurgents.

The repetition of the attack patterns, type of targets, together with failure of officers to defend themselves were both enthralling and shocking. Surrounded by these events, I wanted to learn more about these attacks—particularly since this area has always been my research interest and expertise.

A few weeks into my investigative research, I ran into a friend from high school (2002–2004) who I had not seen in many years. We had a brief discussion as we shared reflections on the complex political situation in Egypt, and he mentioned that something that quickly caught my attention. A mutual friend of ours, Ramy, who attended high school with us, had joined one of the violent anti-government organizations.

I was in absolute shock. The mere fact that one of our old friends enrolled in a violent anti-government organization, and that he is currently characterized a "terrorist/extremist," whether it's true or not, requires significant emotional and mental processing. I wasn't sure what to believe, or rather what to do, especially given the environment of rampant polarization and misinformation. We continued the short conversation, as we mainly reflected on the circumstances that could possibly push someone like Ramy to join these groups.

After this brief conversation, I couldn't stop thinking for a moment about Ramy's transformation. Assuming that this is true, Ramy, someone I shared a bench with throughout my scholastic career, was not the typical suspect of much of the literature on terrorism. What happened to him? And what could possibly transform such a nice, kindhearted person into a violent aggressor?

To make it even more challenging and confusing, as I embarked on my preliminary research into Ramy's violent radicalization, I realized that Ramy was not a rare exception of radicalization. Hundreds of young Egyptians had fled their hometowns to join radical violent groups. Some were friends, and some were friends of friends and others were young people that I have no connection to, but their stories are strikingly similar to Ramy's. Particularly, those who participated in the 2011 mass protests as nonviolent demonstrators. What is that that happened between 2011 and 2013 that could possibly transmute individuals that deep, that fast?

And if many of the once nonviolent Egyptian protesters became violent insurgents, why did this happen only happened to some of them?

Although the field of radicalization witnessed an influx of research in the aftermath of 9/11 attacks to answer similar questions, the exploration remains highly theoretical, with a special focus primarily from security-studies scholars. Despite the recent increase in scholarship, there was a great shortage of empirical studies and firsthand data collection, especially from high-risk places. Additionally, the recent wave of violent radicalization in Egypt was so recent that the existing literature was either deficient or was still in early development stages.

I started to dig into all material I could lay my hands on; articles, interviews, statistics, data, books, and other material. But quickly realized looking for answers in this sort of material a) wouldn't be enough, and b) would not lead to any new explanations—as these have already failed to provide reasonable answers.

I decided that the best way to find an answer was to talk to Ramy himself and find out what happened to him. Listen to him and his motivations rather than reading outdated material that barely touches the reality of this growing phenomenon of radicalization.

I understood that this was not an easy research—nor did I expect it to be. But it was possible, and I was eager to embark on this challenge to the best of my abilities.

What started as an inquisitive, low-priority, project quickly became a full-fledged, very intense research agenda. I was not just driven by curiosity of a friend, but by an urge to understand this growing phenomenon among once hopeful nonviolent pro-democracy activists. Not simply why they were radicalized, but also, how?

Between 2014 and 2020, almost six years of continuous work, I conduct interviews, analysis, debates, travel, and exposure to risky situations that led to the production of this modest book. This book is based on true stories from eyewitness accounts and firsthand reports.

Over the duration of this research, I have conducted numerous interviews with political activists, radicalized individuals, police officers, military officers, state officials, lawyers, scholars, experts, and other stakeholders in an effort to provide a comprehensive understanding of the phenomenon of radicalization.

It is important to note that this study relied on multiple interviews but for the sake of this book and to make the publication simpler and more reader friendly, I selected three interviews with three different representative characters—each encapsulating a blend of the data points I have collected—to serve as the research sample. The exact method of communication with all anonymized interviewees will remain undisclosed. Some of the stories have been slightly modified to disguise the real personas and to avoid their identifications for the safety of their families, friends, and relatives.

Establishing Trust

Shortly after starting my research, I was able to plan safe and secure means to conduct the interview with Ramy.[1] The most challenging step was not to construct a series of questions for the interview or to plan the discussion points, but to establish and maintain an atmosphere of trust where Ramy would willingly share his story. While I knew there would be challenges, there were a few important factors that helped facilitate the interview process.

The most important factor was my previous acquaintance with Ramy. While a relationship between the researcher and the research subject can be seen by some positivist scholars as problematic because the bias of the researcher could influence the conversation, thereby altering the findings (Douglas and Carless 2012), others contend that emotional reflexivity can be a stable bridge between the ethnographic researcher and the interviewee (e.g., Hochschild 1983; Brackenridge 1999; Hoffman 2007; Allen-Collinson and Owton 2014).

Friendship enables us to be "in the world" of others (Tillmann-Healy 2003) where there is common ground that facilitates our understanding of research subjects' unique conditions. It is described by Rawlins (1992) as "an interpersonal bond characterized by the ongoing communicative management of dialectical tensions, such as those between idealization and realization, affection and instrumentality, and judgment and acceptance."

In this case, although my friendship with Ramy was old and brief, it provided a familiar basis of trust and confidence that allowed Ramy to speak spontaneously and candidly. Perhaps he thought that our previous friendship would make me more likely than others to understand his position. Or maybe it was because we had experienced political turmoil together—from Mubarak's days of oppression all the way to 2011's mass protest. Whatever the reason, Ramy's preestablished trust in me was a key in excavating facts and impressions. I invited more open conversations by weaving in personal questions about his life and his family, his emotions, and other influences that could have helped to explain his radicalization. Additionally, gaining Ramy's trust would mean that I could potentially be trusted by Ramy's peers who had similarly taken a path of radicalization.

While I had a million questions, the main one was clear: How, why, and under what conditions do activists in Egypt switch from nonviolent to violent insurgency? Particularly, why did some people, like Ramy and his peers, switch their strategies, while many others remained nonviolent?

But while Ramy is a key interviewee to my study, I can't rely on his input, alone to validate my research. Such a study is complex, interdisciplinary, and requires additional inputs from other potentially radicalized individuals, state officials, experts, etc. Yet due to the delicate nature of the study, I had very little control over choosing whom to interview, especially among radicalized individuals. So, I resorted to an exponential nondiscriminative snowball sampling technique as it was the best option to navigate through this clandestine community. In this technique, Ramy provided a few referrals to individuals who I then interviewed and asked for further referrals.

Although the semistructured interviews had very similar questions for every interviewee, there was a level of flexibility and adaptability I used to collect as much data as possible. This approach allowed for better data and more information that could be analyzed in a later stage, especially when observing the past trajectories and experiences of each radicalized individual. The main idea of the side-by-side comparison is to be able to identify the most salient triggers of transformation and radicalization and analyze them against existing theories.

Despite the unusual conditions and the difficult nature of the project, I managed to interview every subject individually and privately to ensure confidentiality. Conducting interviews individually enabled the subjects to speak more freely and independently of other sources of influence, and to ensure that their real identities won't be revealed.

But it is also important to note that interviews were not the only source of data; I also used other methods like conceptual content analysis, ethnography, and secondary data analysis. I have spent a considerable amount of time examining the media statements issued by a variety of homegrown insurgent groups in the period between 2011 until 2019 looking at linguistic patterns, aspirations, keywords, recruitment strategies, and how they presented themselves to the society. The content sample was exhaustive; it included social media platforms like Facebook, Twitter, YouTube, and other affiliate websites and communication platforms.

Given my background as both an activist and a scholar, I will be approaching these questions from two perspectives. The first lens is that of an activist, and the other is of an academic researcher. While I might be fairly independent as a researcher or academician seeking to determine why the course of events unfolded the way they did, I am not completely detached from the accumulation of events and interactions of forces on the ground I experienced as an activist. I was part of the mass uprising in Egypt in 2011; I have worked closely with multiple politicians, statesmen, and activists from 2005 until the date of writing this book; and thus, I have my own practical experience of the field which has attached me to two different realms: an *activist* and a *researcher* simultaneously.

And while this is considered a challenge for some researchers because it can introduce a challenge when trying to maintain neutrality and integrity throughout the research, it is not an impasse. Michael Peter Smith's (1994) "cultural bifocality" and DuBois's (1994) "double consciousness" explained how people can be involved simultaneously in more than one culture while fully living in neither. "Always looking at oneself through the eyes of others, of measuring one's soul by the tape of a world that looks on in amused contempt and pity" (DuBois 1994, 29).

This cleft identity of the two different cultures (a researcher and an activist) does not undermine my research; in fact, it helps to shed light on new aspects and reveal new perspectives I am sensitive to and have more understanding of, particularly the emotions and aspirations involved. It's an aspect of this type of action that the unfamiliar, detached researcher might overlook. It helped me ask certain questions, share thoughts on politics where necessary but maintained my independence.

RAMY

Ramy wasn't my closest friend in high school, but we shared the same bench for two years (2003–2004). He was very well-mannered, quiet, and dedicated to his studies, and came from a fairly wealthy family. In our class, Ramy was a role model for success and dedication, and always dreamed of being a businessman, following his late father.

Since leaving high school, I only saw Ramy a few times and always at public gatherings. The last time I ran into him was on January 28 during the 2011 mass protests in Alexandria where he was, like myself and many other nonviolent protesters, chanting against the long-standing dictator, Hosni Mubarak.

During this protest we had a chance to chat about the political situation in Egypt at the time. He, in his own words, was not part of any political party or movement. He was just eager to see some political change happen in Egypt so decided to join the protest. January 28, the third day of the nation-wide protest, things turned toward some violence, so our chats were often interrupted by either police-fired tear gas canisters or to escape police's mass arrests and street beating. We would eventually regroup with other protesters and resume our rallying demonstrations. Despite some violent confrontations, Ramy, myself, and many other protesters did not engage in any form of violent activity. In fact, Ramy was most careful to stay out of any zones where the protesters were throwing rocks at the police or vandalizing any of the police vehicles.

Fast forward to my interview with Ramy for the topic of this book, when I sat down with my old acquaintance to begin asking questions, before I was able to say one word, Ramy blurted out: "I am not a terrorist!"[2]

"I never said you were," I replied.

The preemptively defensive position that Ramy took from the start was indictive of his mental and psychological status that seemed to be under an immense pressure to exonerate himself of any wrongdoing as if he was talking in a court of law. Such an interview climate wasn't going to be helpful. I am neither a prosecutor pressing charges against him nor am I an attorney defending him. I am just a researcher, and for this interview to be productive, I have to create a less intense atmosphere.

To reset the conversation, I first redirected our focus to reminiscing about "the good old days" of school to soften the stiffness of the situation. Drawing some laughs by recalling memories from high school, mutual classmates, and teachers. Just like many other teens, high school days were packed with memories and experiences. It didn't matter whether these were good or bad, recalling them was a breeze—especially our constant attempts to flee the school by jumping off the eight- or nine-foot-high fence. Ramy wasn't really known for his good escaping skills, so he required a lot of assistance from our other classmates—which was often a matter of teasing and laughter for everyone.

Our high school times were pretty relaxed. Unlike many other public schools in Egypt, our class wasn't condensed. We were approximately nineteen students in a class that typically would have had more than fifty students, which allowed for more connection between those of us in the class. We shared a bench, which also means we joined in an interesting array of uncanny stuff. Nothing dangerous (or illegal), but certainly things that teachers weren't amused with.

I spoke about myself, my career, some developments in my life and continued to share some of my political views on the situation in Egypt. Expressing my criticism to the military regime prompted Ramy to relax and share some of his views on the political situation in Egypt as well, which naturally helped the conversation to flow where I planned it to. I was careful not to push for any questions or raise any issue that could create tension and distress. Building and maintaining confidence was more important to me than getting the answers to my questions at this point.

My preliminary impression was quite nonconclusive. Rapport wise, it appeared to me that Ramy was the very same person I'd known in high school. Smart, decent, sharp, and a very well-spoken person. I was honestly struggling throughout the conversation to pinpoint or detect the traditionalist red flags I was looking for or some signs of religious fundamentalism—of which I found none.

A noticeable change of his tone, however, was apparent when mentioning issues related to the police. Many Egyptians suffer issues with police—for one reason or another—but the distinct pitch in Ramy's voice when mentioning the police indicated something bigger than general frustration or irritation. His comments were mainly about police's violent practices and the failure of the justice system to either correct this malpractice or to hold those involved in violations accountable. It wasn't clear what the cause of Ramy's strong reaction was, but I knew it was an issue I would come back to explore at a future point.

Despite different presidents, police in Egypt played a central role in political life. They are tasked with missions beyond their constitutional duties; particularly those with political nature such as suppressing opposition groups and mitigating risks associated with political dissent, co-opting media figures, controlling elections, etc. (Amnesty 2012).

Ramy called them "the arms and legs" of the successive dictators in Egypt. "Their sole loyalty is not to a nation, constitution, religion, not even to their own institution. It is only to the sitting president," said Ramy who continued to explain his theory that any political change must first start with a transitional accountability for police's crimes, and then a full-scale reform—even if resorting to violence is necessary.

"Why do we need to engage violence?" I asked.

"Because nonviolence did not work," he answered.

"Did you try to make it work?" I added.

"We both tried," he replied, referring to our participation in the January 2011 mass protest that led to the removal of the Egyptian president, Hosni Mubarak. With exception to a few violent incidents, the uprising was mostly a peaceful expression of opposition to Mubarak's regime.

Mubarak, who assumed power in 1981 after the assassination of former President Anwar El Sadat, deployed coercive tactics to consolidate his regime and ensure his reign for years. His era (1981–2011) was characterized with corruption, nepotism, repression, and police state practices where only his party—the ruling National Democratic Party—fully controlled all arms of government, including the political scene. "Mubarak domesticated the political arena and minimized any threats that could potentially undermine his rule" (Hendawy 2015). His regime mastered the use of different violent and nonviolent maneuvers to maintain his power. Possibilities of social change and mobilization were rare, if not entirely nonexistent. Decades of repression created a political dynamic where opposition groups were either co-opted, cooperative with the state, or simply too weak to pose any threat on the regime.

Systematic violence, coercion, and military trials were complemented by co-opting several opposition figures and movements. Even movements that were too big to be co-opted as a whole weren't far from negotiating political arrangements with state actors. During the 2010 parliamentary elections, Mohamed Morsi, the Muslim Brotherhood elections coordinator at the time [later would be elected president], said "we have secured arrangements with security agencies and with National Democratic Party figures" (Ashour 2013).

The suffocating atmosphere of repression and injustice, combined with the absence of civil and political liberties, were catalysts in encouraging pro-democracy activists to organize, mobilize, and seek the necessary resources in order to change the rigid status quo. Such a circumstance necessitates the rise of some sort of civil resistance movement, if the necessary resources and political openings are there, that will lead to social change and establish alternative patterns of activism.

In 2004 and 2005 the mounting Western pressures forced former President Hosni Mubarak to carry out limited political changes that included constitutional amendments and electoral reforms, which allowed new social movements and political parties to emerge and organize within this very limited space. While groups are central to social movements, it is the deliberately formed associations that play a critical role in creating and sustaining national social movements—and maintaining its nonviolent nature.

The emergence of a national social movement was due to individuals asserting their rights to organize, assemble, and demonstrate within a narrow political space. Furthermore, it was established specifically to accomplish a set of political ends. This was facilitated by the introduction of the new media (e.g., Facebook, v-blogging, Twitter, etc.). Technology enabled the use of the media to organize and increase the visibility of the movements and make other individuals aware of other common grievances. These tools were also utilized to coordinate and sustain collective action, build solidarity, spread movements to new audiences, and transmit information. New media also helped in the transnational diffusion of nonviolent strategies and tactics through years of training and the consulting of the Serbian CANVAS activists to Egypt's April 6 movement, which played a key role in mobilization and organization of the 2011 upraising.

As a result of these changes, opposition movements like Kefaya—which translates as "enough"—emerged in 2004 as a platform to challenge Mubarak's regime and to shake the political stagnation. Similarly, the Al Ghad Party was founded in late 2004 and became an important competitor in the 2005 presidential election. A few years later, in 2008, the April 6 Youth Movement was founded and became a prime actor in Egypt's political scene.

These movements, alongside the already well-established Muslim Brotherhood, Revolutionary Socialists, and other groups, despite their varying *modus operandi* and ideologies created a momentum that not only challenged Mubarak's regime, but also became an incubator of many activists and subgroups in a relatively short period of time (2004–2011). Together, these groups used different tactics and methods to effectively expose Mubarak's failures and formed the foundation for largely nonviolent collective action.

Until 2010, Ramy wasn't part of any organized political opposition groups. He explained that he was against Mubarak's policies, especially Mubarak's plot to make his son, Gamal, the next president of Egypt but he didn't have enough courage to participate in any of protests, just yet. "The atmosphere just wasn't helpful, and I was not familiar with any of the political groups," Ramy explained while continuing his passive disapproval of Mubarak. Many of my and Ramy's generation who were born in the 1980s grew up to see Mubarak as the only president. His photos were everywhere, in every government facility, in every sports club, in every school, sometimes even in classrooms. National TV—mind that this was '80s, '90s, and early 2000s—still largely shaped the public conscience. It was permissible for some papers to criticize the government, but Mubarak and his family remained a strong bold redline (Essa 2009). Political parties were weak, opposition groups were fragmented, disorganized, and barely known to anyone outside their close circles, and going into an anti-government protest would almost certainly land you in jail. Thus, for Ramy and many other young Egyptians, the idea of removing Mubarak was just not fathomable.

But the image of Mubarak's tough regime was about to change. In June 2010, a young man from the coastal city of Alexandria—where Ramy lived—named Khaled Said, was murdered by two police officers while in their custody (*Al-Dustour News*, June 23, 2010). Khaled's murder news went viral and resonated with many people, especially the young population. Ramy stated that Khaled's tragedy moved something in him and encouraged him to take an action to reform the police's increasing corruption. Local activists started to call for anti-police protest in Alexandria and this movement started to snowball and gain more traction.

Ramy's first political activity was to participate in Khaled Said's silent demonstration in Alexandria. The mobilization that took place after Khaled Said's murder was central in building momentum toward political change in Egypt in 2010/2011. Social movements, especially newly formed ones, have played a significant role in recruiting new activists—who were not necessarily politicized or affiliated with a particular political ideology.

The movements surrounding Khaled Said's death provided unique opportunities for people to voice their concerns and grievances, launch claims, organize, and create space for the construction of social movements. The nonviolent momentum was visibly growing, not only new participants, but also new grievances. What started as a campaign to hold the two police officers that were involved in the killing of Khaled Said accountable, quickly escalated to be a call for nationwide police reform.

In this uphill battle against the state, activists used every possible means of nonviolent resistance to voice concerns and challenge the ruling regime. These techniques included judicial procedures, political pressure, popular mobilization, street rallies, advocacy, and many others. But these traditional techniques were ineffective. Courts, parliament, syndicates, and the press were all co-opted by the regime. Senior judges often rise to their positions in supreme courts only when the regime is confident in their loyalty. Parliament, municipal, and syndicate elections are carried out under tight control of the regime. Such co-optation by state made any attempts to use these mechanisms to resist the authoritative military regime hopeless at worst, ineffective at best.

The rise of high-speed internet, however, was a game changer (Khamis and Vaughn 2013). Because of the internet—which was uncensored at the time, activists could get their own censorship-free platform to communicate and express their opinions, plans, and to spread their word to like-minded peers in and outside of Egypt. More importantly, such a space was, at first, mostly uncharted by the government, which was an advantage that activists had over governmental agencies. Technologically savvy activists made excellent use of such a space and started to articulate their opinions, brainstorm solutions, inspire each other, and more importantly form networks among each other— that would come into play at a later stage.

Even when the government hurriedly started to explore this new cyberspace in late 2010, and tried to establish some informal presence, it lagged far behind younger generations' ability to leverage this new platform for their benefit. Lacking the background knowledge about how to leverage the internet and social media, the government was in no position to control it in those early days.

January 25, 2011, Mass Mobilization

After almost six months of small sporadic protests the "We Are All Khaled Said" Facebook page created an event calling on Egyptians to take to the street to protest police brutality in the national day of police: January 25, 2011. The plan was to rally in several cities in Egypt to protest police practices, corruption, demand the removal of Habib Al Adly, the nation's chief of police, limiting presidential terms to only two terms, as well as annulling state of emergency[3] (Ghonim 2012). The invitation spread quickly and was supported by several other groups including the April 6 Movement, Kefya, Ghad Party, National Association for Change, as well as individual public figures.

The marches rolled down the streets, picking up more people as the rallies advanced. Chants became louder, stronger, and the demands became bolder. And while the protests were in several cities in Egypt, Cairo's Tahrir Square captured the most attention and media coverage—and later would become the beating heart of the uprising and its icon.

As the headcount grew larger, especially in Cairo, protesters almost filled the square,[4] police forces raided the square in an attempt to clear it from protesters and take control of it. And while police managed clear the square from the protesters and take control of it late in the evening of January 25, protesters renewed their call for further demonstrations throughout the country. In his book "*Revolution 2.0* (2012), Wael Ghonim, the administer of the Facebook Page that called for the protest, stated: despite the fact that the police took control of the square that night, January 25 wasn't the end, it was the beginning" (Ghonim 2012, 288).

The subsequent days of the protest witnessed excessive state violence against the protesters and police deployed different tactics in an attempt to halt the advances of the movement and prevent it from gaining more support. Almost every trick on the book was used to circumvent the movement; from using lethal violence against protesters all the way to shutting down the internet and cell phone networks to prevent protesters from calling on more support or communicating with the outside world. Yet despite the extraordinary measures, the movement continued to proliferate.

Tahrir Square, the icon and center of the uprising, became a pilgrimage destination where all political parties, despite their differences in ideologies and political leanings, would merge into one just cause: to bring down the regime and bring about a new modern and democratic state. The square became a safe zone to discuss and debate topics that were once taboo without the fear of being arrested or persecuted. Freedom, change, and social justice were the three demands that the activists, of all political affiliations, kept chanting and pushing for, around the clock. I believe there was no force that would have been powerful enough to move protesters out of the square or make them give up their cause at that moment. The more the protesters were attacked, the more resilient and determined they were to bring an end to the Mubarak era.

After eighteen days of unremitting, tenacious protests, the long-standing dictator finally stepped down giving hope to pro-democracy movements across the region. I still remember how it felt when Mubarak stepped down. I was in Tahrir Square, near Talaat Harb Street when we heard the news. Omar Soliman, the then vice president appeared on national TV to announce Mubarak's decision to step down. There were so many of us grouped around a small, tiny TV screen trying to listen carefully and anxiously to every word Soliman was saying. And before he finished his speech, the news was confirmed, and the square erupted in celebration with fireworks and chants.

Nothing can even begin to describe the feeling of euphoria that moved the entire square—and subsequently, the country. Happiness was not the only shared emotion among activists; we felt pride, dignity, and a sense of belonging to a country where we had long been oppressed, as if people were suddenly reconnected with their lost sense of dignity. I remember snapping a photo of a protester who was holding a banner that said: "Finally, I am proud to be an Egyptian." He explained to me that he felt "counted" and that he had enough courage now to be a proud Egyptian.

This utopian sensation swelled dramatically. Youth groups started to organize campaigns to raise awareness of political rights and encourage citizens to register to vote and become active participants in building the country they dream of. Youth from each neighborhood started to volunteer to clean their streets, collect the trash, guard their property until a new government assumed these responsibilities and services had been restored.

"That was it, Mubarak is gone," said Ramy before he quickly added, "or at least I was naïve enough to think so."

The Counterrevolution

Ramy was not the only one to believe in the moment. Many Egyptians thought deposing Mubarak would usher in the beginning of a new era that would be characterized with diversity, pluralism, freedoms, and rule of law. This belief was bolstered in the early days following Mubarak's fall as new political parties, along with older movements like the Muslim Brotherhood and others engaged in a transition to democracy.

But it is important to note that, when Mubarak stepped down, he yielded the governance credentials of the country to the Supreme Council of Armed Force (SCAF). Meaning that, the SCAF, chaired by Egypt's Minister of Defense, who was handpicked and appointed by Hosni Mubarak in 1991 and remained loyal to him ever since, would be directing and overseeing the country's transition to democracy.

Having SCAF, whose members were vigorously vetted for their loyalty to Mubarak, to steer the country to a democratic system where they [the military generals] would give up their privileges, voluntarily, raised a lot of suspicion among pro-democracy activists. Yet despite the skepticism, the situation did not change. The military was the only standing institution that could carry out the transition during this state of turmoil. Besides, activists were overly confident that if the military failed to shepherd in a new democratic order—they could simply mobilize once again and take to the streets to correct the situation.

Shortly after Mubarak stepped down, SCAF—being the *de facto* ruler—made a series of political decisions would confirm the skepticism that pro-democracy activists once had. "Revolutions are nothing but chaos and disorder, yet our job here is to maintain law and order and clean up this mess," said *then* Air Marshal Reda Hafez, Commander of the Air Forces, with a very aggressive tone during a closed meeting I attended in March 2011—days after the military engaged in their first violent clashes with the pro-democracy activists in Tahrir Square. This clash led to arrest of many activists—including eighteen women activists who later would undergo what is known as "virginity tests" by the military prison guard ("The testimony of Rasha Abdul Rahman for virginity tests in the military prison" 2012). Rasha Abdel Rahman, one of the women activists arrested that day explained that all women detainees were asked to strip down naked and forced to undergo a test to ensure that they were virgin girls. "If you state that you are virgin, and we later proved that you were not, we will electrocute you, beat you, and [rape you]," said Ibrahim the solider at the Military Prison as per Rasha's testimony. Abdel Fattah El Sisi, who was at the time the head of the military intelligence, admitted that the military indeed carried out these tests in order to prevent any allegations that these women were raped during their imprisonment in the military prison (*Deutsche Welle News* June 27, 2011).

The clashes, the arrests, and the scandal of the virginity tests on women activists left an astounding impact on political forces—especially those who were already skeptical of the military's intentions and ability to handle the transitional period. Less than ten days after this incident Egyptians were scheduled to vote on a controversial constitutional amendment put forward by the Supreme Council of Armed Forces known as the "March 19 Referendum" ("Egyptian Election Commission" 2011). The amendments included putting a limit on the presidency to two terms, mandating independent judicial oversight of all elections, appoint a commission to draft a new constitution. While all political parties agreed, in principle, that the proposed amendments are a step toward democracy, opponents argued that it is much better to write a new democratic constitution from scratch than putting band-aids on old undemocratic constitution; that way the country goes through a smooth transition while giving enough time for new political forces to organize themselves and prepare for proper elections. Additionally, opponents of the referendum doubted the constitutionality of the procedural process on which the referendum took place.

The referendum controversy together with the violent clashes with activists, the virginity tests scandal, the ambiguity of the transition roadmap created a deep divide between the democratic forces and the military. Many activists started to see the military as part of a "counterrevolution" force that was attempting to circumvent the January 25 uprising and its demands. The dominant rationale among skeptical activists was that the revolution demands essentially pose an existential threat to the military's privileges and political influence, thus the SCAF would never be in favor of a true democratic order where the military has no role in political life or where the generals have to give up their political powers.

The political scene slowly turned into a giant tug of war. While activists viewed the January 25 uprising as a once-in-a-lifetime opportunity to pursue the democratic changes they aspired to, others felt threatened by such a movement. The fear was that it was not only former Mubarak aides and loyalists that would face corruption charges and spend some time behind bars, but that everyone who had enjoyed institutional powers and privileges prior to the January 25 movement was going lose those privileges in the new democratic order. Military officials were in a particularly dire position, having enjoyed a long history of political dominance (since 1952 military officials enjoyed total control of the political process and secured all key state positions for senior military generals and Egyptian presidents—from 1952 until 2011—all grew through the military ranks). Not only did the military gradually become the sole arbiter of all key national matters and an imperative pillar of regime protection and sustainability, but it also grew a massive economic empire yielding an enormous amount of tax-exempt revenue that benefited both the institution and military generals (see Cook 2007; Sayigh 2019).

Zero-Sum Game

Although the strife between the two wings appeared to be between democratic forces versus undemocratic forces, it is important to understand that this struggle was also about survival. Each wing knew that this tug of war was going to end in a zero-sum game; whoever won would end the chances of the other. The thought was, if achieved, an unadorned democracy would eliminate any role for the military in domestic political life. Similarly, if the military dictatorship reinstated itself, the pro-democracy movement and its supporters would land in jail and would lose every progress they made in the democratization process. Thus, each wing silently undermined the existence of the other in an atmosphere of skepticism and distrust, which further complicated the transitional period.

With each incremental win for either the pro-democracy movement or the military, resources and determination increased—further exacerbating the struggle and intensifying the animosity between the two groups. Some observers could undoubtedly argue that the fight was inequitable because the military was in possession of everything it takes to manipulate the situation to their favor: media, security apparatuses, financial institutions, the "legitimate" right to use of force, and most vital entities were all controlled by loyalists to the military wing. However, the military was also destabilized and disrupted by the uprising. Foran (2005) would see this internal disruption of the state (military) coupled with the global context which supported Egypt's pro-democracy movement at the time, as a world systematic opening that created a unique opportunity for the democratic movement and parties to build proper alliances and partnerships to enable a gradual political change and smooth transfer of power. In other words, the military was weakened and unfocused due to internal chaos, so pro-democracy movements had a rare window to organize, build alliances, and act to seize the moment.

Despite this very rare opening, and regardless of the reasons, the pro-democracy movements were distracted, disorganized, muddled, and ultimately failed to seize this moment. Whether it was the formation of the wrong alliances, lack of experience, the overwhelming power of the military or a combination of all of the above, failing to exploit the opportunity thwarted the pro-democracy movements. The groups stumbled and failed to advance their plans, the pro-democracy revolutionary wing was losing, while in turn, the pro-military wing was gaining much political ground.

As the military win gained clout, pro-democracy movement started to crumble and disintegrate. The Muslim Brotherhood, which was one key actor that was seen for the longest part as a pro-democracy participant, was swinging back and forth between the two camps. While technically they were always the traditional opposition organization to the military regimes and did join the January 25 protest (albeit later than most forces), many pro-democracy activists—particularly liberals—disagreed so vehemently with the Brotherhood's positions that they chose to work in favor of the military instead of supporting the Brotherhood's emerging prominence in the new democratic state.

Shorouk,[5] a woman activist stated in an interview that "instead of standing firmly with the revolutionary demands, the Brotherhood took a pragmatic yet very dangerous approach to side with the military on almost every step of the way. From March 19 vote, all the way to finding excuses to the military violence against nonviolent protests in Tahrir Square." Despite her critical opinion of the Muslim Brotherhood, Shorouk voted for Mohamed Morsi in the presidential election because she didn't want to see the military win through Morsi's rival candidate, Ahmed Shafik, Mubarak's last prime minister who was also a former military general.

The political positions of the Muslim Brotherhood—which were seen as disappointing by many pro-democracy activists—created an atmosphere of distrust and agitation that would shape the political process for the years to come. But as the presidential elections approached in 2012, pro-democracy activists met with the Muslim Brotherhood candidate, Mohamed Morsi, in order to form an agreement by which they would vote for him in the presidential runoff if he pledged to fulfill their demands—a convention later referred to as the Fairmont Accords. The Fairmont Accords included demands such as the formation of a inclusive government that involved representatives of all political affiliations, ending political polarization, and appointing a fair and representative committee to write a constitution that would ensure freedoms and rights (Kandil 2012).

One Year of Muslim Brotherhood Rule

On June 30, Mohamed Morsi was sworn in as the first democratically elected civilian president of Egypt. In the months following his election, President Morsi took significant steps to cement and consolidate his power. Some of these steps however were seen as a violation to the Fairmont Accords that was signed between the pro-democracy movement and the Muslim Brotherhood's Mohamed Morsi. His proponents justified some of the measures he took—like issuing a constitutional declaration to immunize his decisions from any lawsuits—as necessary because the judiciary was plagued with Mubarak's loyalists and he needed to take some extraordinary measures to protect the revolutionary demands (see Egyptian Constitutional Declaration 2012).

"I don't know if they were incompetent or hungry for power," said Ramy who has been very critical to Morsi's rule and the Muslim Brotherhood's leadership in general. "They took the parliament, the Presidency, government, the constitution's writing committee, and everything for themselves and became so arrogant," he added. The Brotherhood's failures to accommodate other political fictions started to weigh on the revolution's demands and objectives.

The friction and growing divide among pro-democracy created an opportunity for the military. With the assistance of its influential media outlets, the military went on coordinated campaigns to demonize the January uprising and its figures, slogans, and goals, including the Muslim Brotherhood, as a group and Morsi as a unsuccessful president. TV presenters like Khiary Ramadan, Ahmed Moussa, Lamees Al Hadidi (see YouTube,[6, 7, 8] and others turned on January uprising activists, accusing them of receiving funds from foreign conspirators to undermine national security and destroy the national military. The massive media campaign generated a state of political and social polarization online and on the streets, creating an atmosphere characterized with distrust, enmity, and antagonism (Hendawy 2015).

One year into Morsi's Muslim Brotherhood presidency, polarization was growing and had not ceased since Election Day. Repeated failures on behalf of Morsi and his administration only added fuel to the fire. Debates over the state's religious identity added a religious flavor to the escalating social polarizations and increased the level of popular discontent. The Brotherhood's takeover of governance and their failure to accommodate the insecurities of other liberal and leftist movements created a distance between the Muslim Brotherhood and their fellow revolutionary activists. The growing fractions among the democratic wing only played in favor of the military wing, which quickly exploited the divisions within revolutionaries' factions to drastically change the course of the transition.

Rights groups and leftist movements called on the correction of the "revolutionary path" that the Muslim Brotherhood leadership deviated from. Khaled,[9] a political activist, said the call for a large-scale protest against the MB was an absolute necessity because their behavior in both the parliament and the president's office were nothing but a complete betrayal to the January demands—that were never met.

The momentum picked up and many people took to the street on June 30, 2013, to express their dissatisfaction with the one-year rule of the MB President Mohamed Morsi. Whether this anti-Morsi/anti-MB movement was engineered by, or at least supported by the military generals, is and will continue to be a matter of a dispute and debate.

The anti-Morsi demonstrations that started on June 30 and continued for a few days were met by an opposing wave of pro-Morsi supporters. Each group occupied a few public squares, set their camping gear up, and recalled all their protest skills from January 2011. But this time, unlike January 2011, when all of them were united in one cause, they turned against one another.

Head over Heels

On July 3, 2013, the battle for power took a perilous turn when the military generals stepped in, in their uniforms, and declared a coup d'état, removing the Muslim Brotherhood–elected president and replacing him with a military-backed interim government. Abdel Fattah El Sisi, who was appointed by Mohamed Morsi less than one year earlier as a Minister of Defense, appeared on national TV and claimed that the removal of the elected president was indispensable and that it "was the duty of the Egyptian Armed Forces to act in accordance with its patriotic and historic responsibility."

Within hours, pro-military media outlets and influential figures backed the generals' move and depicted the coup d'état as a necessity to "save" the nation from the immense threat to national security and imperative to the stability of Egypt. Shortly after the declaration, ousted President Mohamed Morsi was placed under house arrest with many of his top aides and cabinet members.

The military, which became the *de facto* ruler and governor of the state, launched a belligerent campaign to silence any and all individuals and organizations that expressed their disagreement with the military coup.

A central security police officer interviewed on the conditions of anonymity said that the commands arrived from the office of the Minister of Interior (the nation's police chief) on the evening of July 3, which directed special units to carry out targeted missions to be executed before the morning of the following day. He explained that the list his unit received contained names of twelve individuals (mostly Islamists) to be arrested. The commands warned that these individuals could be armed and may engage in violence. The officer stated that he located and arrested only one of the twelve names, and no arms or weapons were found on the scene.

A full-scale assault began on the short gains of the January 2011 revolution, including banning anti-coup demonstrations, limiting the movement of NGOs, jailing dissent leadership and activists, shutting down media outlets, and murdering and kidnapping numerous activists, especially those with Islamist affiliations.

The Supreme Council of Armed Forces issued a statement urging its own chairman, Abd el-Fattah Al-Sisi, to run for office and offered its full support and loyalty (Abdel Azim 2014). It was obvious from the exceptional measures that the military took at the time that the military was on their way to reinstating themselves as full leaders of the country and was about to declare the end of the brief democratic spring.

"I was supportive of removing Mohamed Morsi from office, albeit I didn't really like the way he was removed," said Ramy, "although that was probably the only way to remove him."

"I didn't like the way the Muslim Brotherhood governed the country," he said as he explained that "the brotherhood committed some inexcusable violations to the January revolution demands." Such frustration, Ramy explains, was the reason behind his decision to support the removal of Mohamed Morsi. But Ramy was eventually supportive of the military which he had seen as "the only functioning institution" in Egypt at the time—and thus the only capable force of countering the Brotherhood.

Ramy wasn't the only one to think so. Many people and groups—largely with liberal and leftist affiliations—were frustrated with the Muslim Brotherhood for their exclusionary rule and self-centric practices. The June 30 demonstration was a call to take to the street and put pressure on Morsi—and thereby the Muslim Brotherhood—to step down from the office.

Many of those who participated in the June 30 demonstrations were groups and individuals that were also essential in prompting the initial January 2011 revolution, such as the April 6 Movement, Revolutionary Socialists Movement, and Labor Syndicates.

While some of these groups, like the Revolutionary Socialists Movement, refused any military intervention in the removal of Mohamed Morsi, many others chose to support the military in the forceable removal of Morsi. Whether their reasons were enough to legitimize their support to the military in removing an elected president or not is a matter of dispute (El Masry 2013).

Following the coupe, the military seized every chance to bolster their position as a sole governor of the country. Appointing military-backed personnel to run key ministries, agencies, and governorates (*Al-Ahram Online,* August 8, 2013). Simultaneously, the judiciary and prosecution were co-opted to serve the interest of the military junta. Pro-military judges and prosecutors started to tailor arbitrary accusations, and later issued sentences, that went as far as the death penalty (*BBC News* 2014a; El Ansary 2017). The verdicts were random and not based on any proper investigations, to such an extent that military court accidentally sentenced a four-year-old child to life in prison (*BBC News* 2016).

During the Mubarak era, judges often had a limited level of independence allowing them to avoid death penalties or harsh sentences in politically charged cases. However, after the military coup, the judicial system lost the small amount of independence it once had; "it no longer even attempts to uphold the rule of law or administer justice to its citizens; its main purpose now is to protect the state, primarily the army and police" (Kouddous 2015). The judicial process became nothing more than a tool in the hands of the military to issue extreme sentences to anyone who constituted the slightest threat to the ruling military regime. "The judicial system became a killing machine," said Abdel Rahman,[10] a judge interviewed for this book.

Verdicts of mass death penalties became very common. Nagy Shehata, a judge and loyalist to the military regime "has sentenced 204 people to death and doled out 7,395 years in prison to 534 people in just five rulings." Shehata justified sentencing three *Al Jazeera* journalists to jail in 2013, stating that "the devil encouraged them to use journalism and direct it towards actions against the nation" (Kouddous 2015) This level of extreme deceit and nonsense could only be found in the poorly produced drama that was Egypt after 2013.

Judge Abdel Rahman stated in his interview that the military took control of the whole judiciary and imposed a tight grip over it. Judges were frightened to issue any verdict that would dismay the military generals. "If someone was brought to the court under politically motivated charges, he has almost less than 1 percent of fair trial chance," said one judge. Sharif Abdel Kouddous (2015) wrote: "Islamists, activists, human rights advocates, civil society workers, journalists, trade unionists, students, street children and the LGBT community have all been targeted. Meanwhile, police and public officials have received acquittal after acquittal. Despite the killing of hundreds of protesters by security forces, you would be hard pressed to find a single police officer behind bars. Despite the rampant corruption and violence of the Mubarak regime, former government administrators have all been released from prison" (Koudous 2015).

The military's return to power in 2013 was more violent than anyone could have ever imagined. Several independent rights groups have blamed Egypt's security forces for using excessive force, unnecessary gunfire, and failing to protect peaceful protesters during the crackdown on the Rab'aa sit-in, killing hundreds. Similarly, the Grand Imam of Al-Azhar, Ahmed El Tayeb, who initially supported the military coup and attended its statement of declaration, have publicly denounced the bloodbath and said, "We, in AlAzhar were not part of and were not informed of any intent to violently disperse the pro-Morsi at the Rab'aa sit-in" (El Tayeb 2013).

The Cairo Institute for Human Rights Studies also condemned the disproportionate use of force and lethal violence by Egyptian security forces when dispersing the sit-in of protesters at Rab'aa al-Adawiya and Nahda squares. The Institute's report says "[t]he actions left hundreds dead and thousands seriously injured, as well as dozens of bodies torched in still unexplained circumstances. We believe the security apparatus could have avoided this human tragedy if it had complied with international rules and standards for the dispersal of assemblies. Moreover, in the past weeks, the security authorities have failed to do their duty to take the necessary legal measures to protect public security and citizens, particularly residents and passersby in the aforementioned two areas" (Statement and Position Papers 2013).

A state of shock swept the country in just a matter of days. Whether pro-military or against it, the crackdown was so large that nearly everyone in Egypt was influenced by the events of one day or another. The military's actions to slam down the democratic aspirations were extraordinarily vehement and unrelenting. This resulted in the death, arbitrary arrest, torture, and imprisonment of many nonviolent political activists who once sought and worked for achieving democratic reforms. Moreover, and more importantly, the space of political participation, let alone civil resistance, contracted dramatically, to the extent that the very idea of political process in Egypt seemed either hazardous or an off-limit taboo.

The Spark

Ramy's nuclear family (mother and brother) were supporters of the military in general and the Field Marshal Abdal Fattah Al-Sisi in particular. They were like many Egyptians, more concerned about stability and safety of the country and their families than in democratic ideals and political pluralism. Despite Ramy's growing concern over the military violence against pro-Morsi supporters he decided to keep a low profile and stay out of confrontation so that he could focus on his graduate studies and make sure he provided for his mother and younger brother's education.

After the military junta took control of the country, Ramy's low profile life did not witness any major events. Mornings were usually spent either at work, or on campus when he had lectures to attend and school assignments to turn in. Evenings were routinely reserved to meet with neighborhood friends near his home where they would spend their time between drinking tea and coffee, smoking flavored shisha—if they had some money to spare—playing FIFA in a PlayStation rental nearby.

But this monotonous routine was just about to change forever. One day Ramy was staying late at work to catch up on some tasks when he received what he described as "the worst and shortest phone call in his life." The call transcript read as "your brother has been arrested and we don't know where he is."

"It was as if you poured down a bucket of ice on my head," Ramy said. "I was shaking, my knees were trembling, and my heartbeat could be heard from a kilometer away."

The distance from where Ramy works and where he lives is about thirty minutes walking distance. He went back home running, not paying attention to traffic, people, or any road hazards. "All I wanted to know was where my brother was and what had happened."

Ramy developed a strong bond with his younger brother since the passing of his father. Ramy found himself responsible for his brother's well-being and became a mentor to him. "I would take him to school, help him in the homework, and when he grew a little, we used to share clothes."

Ramy's neighbor witnessed the arrest and briefed him on what he had seen. The police arrested Ramy's brother because they assumed he was a participant in a pro-Muslim Brotherhood demonstration that was rallying through the main street—where Ramy's family live.

Ahmed, Ramy's younger brother, had absolutely no relation whatsoever to politics. It was a matter of coincidence that Ahmed happened to be crossing the street headed to his home, when the police attempted to disperse the pro-Morsi demonstration and wrongfully assumed that Ahmed with part of it.

When Ramy and his mother knew the reason for the arrest, they were confident that if they filed a complaint about the wrongful arrest, the police would stand corrected and Ramy's brother would be cleared to go. Ahmed had no political affiliation, had never been involved in one before, and he was simply too young to pose any threat to the government.

Unfortunately, their expectations were wrong. At the police station, Ramy and his mother were denied entry, cussed at, and warned that if they showed up at the police station again, they would be "thrown behind the sun."[11] But the family never gave up their faith in fair treatment. They then approached the Itahadia Presidential Palace, the residence of the then newly elected President Abdel Fattah Al-Sisi, to file another complaint. However, here their expectations didn't just fail, they were shattered, as Ramy's mother was grabbed violently by her arm by one of the police sergeants who had rejected her pleas to meet the president or any of his senior aides to inquire about her son's case. When Ramy attempted to defend his mother, he was placed under arrest and sent to the police detention center.

When Ramy was transported directly to what he thought was prison, on charges of which he wasn't informed and without seeing a lawyer, a prosecutor, or a judge, explains, "I was scared to death. It was so unreal that I kept hoping it was just a bad nightmare—except that it wasn't."

Ramy spent the majority of his first ten days in solitary confinement. The only time he would be out of this cell was for questioning and interrogation. Questioning would happen on random times and was always with his eye's blindfolded and hands sometimes tied to his legs.

After four weeks of detention, Ramy was finally told what he was arrested for and what charges were pending against him. These were "joining a terrorist organization, vandalism, and assaulting public officers during their duty hours." Without seeing a lawyer or given an opportunity to go through the due process, Ramy would now go to be questioned by the prosecutor's office where he was supposed to have an opportunity to explain and defend himself.

"Up until this moment I had a shred of hope that the prosecution will dismiss the charges and let me go, but I was wrong, yet again."

Ramy didn't see a prosecutor that day and was forced to sign documents that stated his confession of plotting against the state and planning to assassinate several state officials. "How I moved from spending a regular day at work, to being a terrorist in just a few days I have no idea," said Ramy with irony in his voice.

Haleem, a human rights lawyer who worked closely on similar cases, said that "with very few exceptions, in these cases prosecutors generally press charges that are pre-fabricated." He explained that State Security prosecutors fall under great influence of the police's national security officers who ultimately make final decisions on these sorts of cases.

Ramy's detention on charges of terrorism landed him in a maximum-security prison. In prison, a whole new chapter in Ramy's life would begin. "Prison is a whole world on its own," said Sameer, a police officer interviewed for this book. Egypt's prisons are notorious, not only for their torture, abuse, and cruelty but also for their overcrowded cells, lack of heath care, and poor sanitary practices.

Ramy would be allocated to one of the overly crowded cells with other political prisoners with similar charges—including those who have received death sentences or life in prison as well as others, like Ramy, who were pending lengthy investigations. Many detainees, Ramy recalls, had pending charges since the military coup in July 2013, all on almost identical charges as Ramy's.

The cell where Ramy was assigned was so overcrowded that prisoners had to organize themselves and take turns on who would have a sliver of floor to sleep. Age, medical conditions, and group affiliations all played a role on where and when to sleep, he explained. In a report by *Deutsche Welle News*, Kristen McTighe (2015) interviewed Ahmed Parsi, a twenty-seven-year-old engineer who was arrested at a protest on June 30, 2013, and spent nearly two years in a cell in Tora prison before being released in late 2015. Parsi recalls "the cell I was in was full of insects and dirty, but we cleaned it and we could survive." Parsi confirmed the overflow of the prison's capacity when he described the cell he was placed in "four-by-five-meter prison cell shared with, on average, fifteen other men. Included inside the cell was a darkened, dirty hole to squat over for a toilet. Prisoners hung a sheet to separate it from the rest of the cell, something that did little to remedy the stench that permeated the cell. With nothing but a crack in the ceiling for a window, he said the summer heat was almost unbearable, as was the cold winter chill. When asked about health care, for those who needed it, he said there was none" (McTighe 2015).

Ramy was also denied even his most basic right: health care. The prison's general practitioner prescribed Ramy a daily medication to treat a chronic health condition that he suffered from that could lead to serious complications if he had not been treated properly and timely. Ramy claims that despite the doctor's clear instructions, the pills were never dispensed to him at any time throughout his months behind the bars, causing Ramy immense suffering and serious deterioration of his health.

Torture is not only limited to inflicting direct physical harm on prisoners by electrocution or twisting knives in their backs, but torture also encompasses the threat of permanent, severe disfigurement, sleep deprivation, preventing prisoners from accessing proper health care, denying personal hygiene products, overriding prisons' original capacity, and other forms of abuses; all which Ramy has stated that he had experienced with varying degrees throughout his imprisonment time. A recent study of nearly 300 survivors of torture from former Yugoslavia showed that prisoners who were subjected only to psychological torture report as much mental anguish as those who had experienced physical torture (Khamsi 2007).

In Egypt, authorities do not shy away from inflicting both physical and psychological harm on their political dissidents. Essam Sultan, an imprisoned senior politician of the Wasat Party testified to in court in a recorded video that he had not received the [trial] referral order, nor was he allowed to see case trial documents, let alone seeing a lawyer. "I am denied access to paper, pen, food, clean water. I am denied everything"[12] said Sultan on May 2016. Similarly, Essam El Arian, a senior member Muslim Brotherhood and a former parliamentarian, said in his testimony to the court,[13] in August 2016, that he had witnessed the death of four inmates as the prison management refused to deliver emergency health care, claiming that, for prison guards, "this is a systematic policy, they deliberately let people die after torture and deny healthcare to them." Essam El Arian added, "they told us; we will slowly kill you here."

One of the most notorious prisons in Egypt is a maximum-security prison called the "Scorpion Prison," which was specifically designed and built for political prisoners. "It was designed so that those who go in don't come out again unless dead," according to Ibrahim Abd al-Ghaffar, former warden, during a television interview in 2012 ("An Interview with Gen. Ibrahim, Director of Scorpion Prison" 2012). General Abd al-Ghaffar's statement is particularly true when examined against the data that shows the number of prisoners who did not leave this prison prior to their death. The list of deceased prisoners includes Essam Derbala of the Islamic Group, who died when prison administration declined emergency health care for him in 2015, Ezzat El Salamony, who died in 2015 due to physical torture, Morgan Salem of the Salafis in 2015, Farid Ismail of the Muslim Brotherhood in 2015, Nabil Maghraby in 2016, and others who faced similar conditions that equally led to their death inside their cell (*Al Watan News* August 10, 2015).

Per multiple independent human rights agencies, approximately 60,000 people have been arrested since August 2013, including liberal activists, Muslim Brotherhood members, human rights lawyers, journalists, and others, and most of them have been referred to the Scorpion Prison, Liman Tora, and other similarly brutal prisons.

Prison Cell: The Combustion Chamber

It is in the dark of the prison cells that many brains, with radical ideas, gravitated toward one another to debate, fight, and discuss the different forms of resistance, but also recruit new calibers, argued Abdel Rahman Ayyash, a researcher who has been working on issues of radicalization in prisons. Ayyash (2019), examined the detention conditions in which the Muslim Brotherhood's youth had been incarcerated in after the 2013 military coup. He observed that a number of the Muslim Brother inmates—including those who were arrested on nonviolent, but still political, charges—ended up joining violent organizations like Islamic State, Al-Qaeda, and other organizations. In his study, Ayyash relegates a significant portion of the MB radicalization to the condition of incarceration, not only how inhumane these conditions are, but also, the mounting pressure that these inmates fall under during their imprisonment and describes it as a multifaceted and comprehensive process.

After spending a few months in prison, Ramy bonded with other inmates that he had not known before. And while many of these inmates, as Ramy recalls, were all well-educated professional young men, they shared something far more significant than education and career accomplishments. A sense of "hopelessness and frustration" stemming from the analogous emotional distress that they experienced over their course of imprisonment.

Political detainees are often exposed to a brutal level of torture and humiliation during their interrogation that is exclusively carried out by National Security Officers in pre-prison/prosecution phase. "We could relate to each other's pain—because we all have been there." Several, former political prisoners' interviewees, have shared in their testimonies that the techniques of interrogations are more or less the same. Intimidation, extortion, beating, hanging, or a combination of all of those at once. After interrogation, we were shattered, drained, and barely able to move—but miraculously, no visible wounds or injuries.

Sameer, the police officer, said that the decades of torture practices in Egypt's detention facilities made the officers master the skills of torturing inmates without leaving visible marks on their bodies like bruises, injuries, or broken bones.

This is exactly what three inmates interviewed for this book have confirmed. The three of them indicated that they could feel an unbearable pain due to the different tactics used, whether electrocution, hanging, or some similar torture, but without—most of the time—locating any sign of injury or bruises. "The motive is not often to extract information," said Major Alaa, an officer interviewed for this study, "but rather inflict pain to humiliate the subject and make them feel helpless and useless."

"I offered to sign any papers or confessions they wanted me to say to avoid torture. But even that would not dissuade them from torturing me," said Ramy. "It's as if they enjoy the process of humiliating us," said Yehia, a twenty-year-old inmate who was also pending investigation of charges on terrorism. When ask if they ever tried to raise complaints against those officers to the prosecutors, judges, or prison administration, the answer, that was often mixed with sarcasm, was yes—and not once or twice, but many times. The response to their complaints varied from denying hearing them all the way to sending them to solitary confinement as a punishment for daring to complain.

Political inmates often live at the mercy—and sometimes the fluctuating mood—of the National Security Officer in charge of their cases. Rule of law, due process, and accountability are almost fictitious afterthoughts that even lawyers can't enforce, to the extent that it's difficult to even document violations against their clients. Human rights lawyer, Haleem H., said, "when a client informs me of any allegations of torture, I have to take it seriously and follow the guidelines—even though I know that would not help improve his situation or lead to holding any officer accountable."

"In the beginning I was adamant about documenting these violations—not just against myself, but against others as well," said Yehia, who also admitted that the repeated failures to his attempts to document the violations made him lose his steam in pursuing or chasing those officers, but also made him "extremely frustrated."

The cruel interrogation practices perpetuated by the security officers created a shared sense of hopelessness among the detainees, especially that the inmates endeavor to document and stop these violations have failed repeatedly leading to nothing but further retaliation by the officers.

Recruiters

Another important observation that can be drawn from all accounts is the timing in which in-prison recruiters approach inmates trying to convince them to join armed groups. Both Ramy and Yehia said they were approached by recruiters right after they returned from interrogation sessions (which often meant they were exposed to varying degrees of torture).

Recruiters, despite their affiliation, were often sympathetic and supportive as described by interviewees. They usd different approaches that varied from ideological and religious jargon all the way to populist narratives to convince and enlist the potential inmate.

"They are good at debating," said Ramy who identified himself as "not so good at religion." Ramy found himself speechless or rather not able to come up with counterarguments against what recruiters said. "We often hear a lot of arguments back and forth especially between ISIL/Al-Qaeda inmates and the Muslim Brotherhood inmates." Researcher Abdel Rahman Ayyash (2019) addressed the debate that takes place in a form of almost shuttle diplomacy between Muslim Brotherhood leaders and ISIL/Al-Qaeda inmates where many young prisoners are squeezed in the middle, listening for all sorts of Fatwas that legitimize or delegitimize concepts of armed rebellion against the state.

While Ayyash's research doesn't indicate there is a winning side in such debates, some data showed that ISIL and Al-Qaeda remains attractive to some youth in prison especially that they have some of the best recruiters who, per multiple interviewees, are highly talented and well-spoken people whose task is spotting potential recruits inside the prison environment. Recruiters then work closely on potential individuals until they are fully indoctrinated and set on the path of embracing radical ideas. Despite the efforts of recruitment, Ramy didn't succumb to any of these endeavors, at least in the beginning.

There is not much known about the *recruiters*, but indeed they know how to choose the right moment to make an approach. There were many harsh and inhuman moments that political detainees live and experience but the most difficult times, Ramy explains, was the moment when one prisoner was taken to be given the death penalty. "It's not that we love each other or necessarily agree with one another's ideas, but we all know that chances are this person being murdered on phony chargers without an opportunity to defend himself, are extremely high," said Ramy before quickly adding, "and we know, any of us, could be next and that is an indescribable moment," added Ramy.

And as if Ramy's compounding tragedy was not enough for him to handle, he soon gets struck with another piece of devastating news. His mother had passed. Her health had rapidly deteriorated due to her agony about the wrongful detention of her only children. The news reached Ramy in prison and it was a shock. He shudders as he recalls these moments with tears, "[t]hose criminals [the police] had no mercy in their hearts; they destroyed my life, jailed my brother, and killed my mother—what is left to look forward to in this life? I am dead alive!"

After a few weeks of his mother's passing, Ramy would be released after prosecution finally decided that there was no sufficient evidence to confirm Ramy's guilt in any of the charges that were pressed against him. But it's too late for him. He had already made up his mind. He will take up arms, fight, and got revenge.

HUSSEIN

Hussein, a young man in his thirties, joined one of the violent groups in Egypt in the aftermath of 2013's military coup. Unlike Ramy, Hussein had been a member of the Muslim Brotherhood since his childhood. He was born into a Muslim Brotherhood family of a conservative political and social worldview. He grew up as an active member of his community, a member of multiple charity organizations, and described himself once as a faithful moderate Muslim.

Hussein said he believed in nonviolent civil resistance so much that he was present from day one of the January 25 revolution despite the MB's leadership instructions that demanded him to avoid protests that day. "This was the 'light at the end of the tunnel' that we used to hear of," Hussein said in reference to the January mobilization, which he saw as a once-in-a-lifetime opportunity to pursue social change. Although Hussein identified himself as a loyal member of the Muslim Brotherhood, he also underlined that he had disagreements with the leadership of the group that favored alignment with the military generals during the transition period. "I voiced my concern against that, but their answer was that what they are doing is 'too sophisticated for me to understand' at the time," said Hussein with a cynical laugh.

"I was always seen as the rebellious boy in the group," said Hussein who explained that he has opposed, internally, many of the Muslim Brotherhood's leadership decisions especially after 2011. Hussein's main point of contestation with the Brotherhood is "unquestionable, unconditional obedience and loyalty" that the group requires above anything else.

"A senior leader in the Muslim Brotherhood called me on November 22, 2012 to ask me to head the Supreme Constitutional Court immediately," said Hussein, who questioned the reason for this request. The senior leader answered, "President Mohamed Morsi will issue a very important decree and we need to mobilize as many people as we can in the court's vicinity to show popular support to the upcoming decree."

"What decree?" asked Hussein.

"We don't know yet, but you need to head there now," replied the senior leader.

Hussein explained that this conversation didn't go well when he refused to support "an important decree" that he had no idea what it was about. "And my sense was right," said Hussein when he later knew that the important decree was the Constitutional Declaration in which President Morsi gave himself "Godlike powers" and protected himself from any judiciary check.

The November Constitutional Declaration sparked an outrage against President Mohamed Morsi and the Brotherhood government. Amr Hamzawy, a prominent scholar and a politician, described the decree in an interview with *The New York Times* that this is "an absolute presidential tyranny" (Kirkpatrick 2012). Even some Islamist figures like Dr. Abdel Moneim Abo ElFottoh said that "passing a revolutionary demand within a package of autocratic decisions is a setback for the revolution" (Kirkpatrick 2012).

The gap between the Muslim Brotherhood and the pro-democracy movement was increasing dramatically. But when liberal and leftist movements called for their anti-Morsi protests on June 30, 2013, the Muslim Brotherhood were pretty lax—at least in the beginning. They were confident that they had the popular support and that nothing would ever remove them from power. I remember a conversation with a senior member of the Muslim Brotherhood's leadership a few days before people took to the streets in June 2013 where he confirmed that there was nothing to worry about and that June 30 "will be the biggest failure there ever was in the history of popular mobilizations."

But June 30 turnout was much bigger than the Brotherhood have anticipated. People started rolling the streets which, in turn, instigated the Muslim Brotherhood leadership to call its members to organize a counterprotest that would show the pro-Morsi support in all cities of Egypt. Despite Hussein's fundamental disagreements with the Muslim Brotherhood's leadership policies, he found himself supporting President Morsi's rallies. "Just because he was an incompetent President, it does not mean that we call on the military to remove him. If we call the military to remove every President that we don't like, then why do we even hold elections?"

Hussein's sentiment of supporting President Morsi, whether for the reasons he stated or simply out of loyalty to the MB, was indeed shared by many other protesters who took to the streets to express their position. Although the majority of Muhammed Morsi's support was evidently from the Muslim Brotherhood, he also had some significant support from other Islamist factions.[14]

While the pro-Morsi had multiple locations (mainly in Cairo but also in other cities in Egypt) where they gathered to express their support for President Morsi, two locations gained more momentum than any other: Rab'a Al Adawya Square in East Cairo and El Nahda Square in Giza. Rab'a Square in particular was more significant as it was much spacious and closer to the Itihadya Presidential Palace.

The Rab'a protester grew larger, and protesters started to set up tents, sleeping bags, a stage, and a media station as they prepared for what seemed to be a long and arduous sit-in. The situation escalated rapidly and reached a point of a political impasse. Violent confrontation broke out among the pro- and anti-Morsi protesters when they were in close geographical proximity to each other, while the general political scene remained tense.

In less than five days following the June 30 protests, the Supreme Council of Armed Forces (SCAF) declared their decision to forcibly remove Mohamed Morsi on July 3, 2013. They suspended the constitution (*Al-Ahram News* July 3, 2013a) declared a state of emergency (*Al-Ahram News* August 14, 2013b), closed all critical media outlets and satire shows (*Deutsche Welle News* July 24, 2013) and eventually designated the Muslim Brotherhood as a terrorist organization.

The military bold decision to remove the elected president sent shockwaves across the political spectrum in Egypt while its ripple effects could be seen regionally and internationally. Several local and international actors including Catherine Ashton, the High Representative of the European Union for Foreign Affairs and Security Policy, engaged in efforts to defuse the congested, and rapidly escalating, political crisis but with very little progress.

Meanwhile Rab'aa sit-in became the icon of resistance to the pro-Morsi crowds. The more complicated the situation became, the more Rab'aa became a safe haven to its crowd—or so the pro-Morsi protesters thought. Gradually, pro-Morsi rallies and crowds started receiving attack after attack—wherever they were. Pro-Morsi protesters blamed undercover police and "paid" thugs for carrying out these attacks. Hussein, who used to go to Rab'a every day and still preferred to sleep in his bed at home, had been told by his friends that they needed him to be present in the Rab'a at all times. As a physician, he was a valuable asset to help setting up a field hospital—which runs basically like a small emergency room in case any protesters need medical attention—especially that Rab'a Square had already been a target of violent attacks by anti-Morsi crowds. "I was ready to help in any way possible—although I really hoped we wouldn't reach this point," said Hussein.

In the same field hospital was another young physician—a recent graduate—volunteering to help with medical emergencies: his name is Saeed. One of Saeed's closest friends, who had known Saeed since their childhood was interviewed for this book. He described Saeed as a handsome, shy, and a very sensitive person. "Simply a sweet person," said his friend, who also said that Saeed was very popular among schoolteachers when he was young. He spent a few years in Europe with his family but moved at a young age to Egypt where he grew up in a small city in Egypt's Nile Delta among his Muslim Brotherhood family. He was a moderately religious person "but in no way was he proselytizing violence or hostile ideas against any one or any groups" said his friend.

Saeed was also a talented artist and painter. And despite a major accident that caused some serious injuries during his high school years, he was able to recover and score high enough on his exams so he could attend medical school.

On July 8, 2013, the holy month of Ramadan began, a month that everyone hoped would bring some peace to the negotiations table between pro-Morsi and the ruling military junta. Instead, the month just witnessed failure after failure in negotiations that were mediated by several international figures. All led to the same result: nothing.

The whole month of Ramadan was an opportunity for negotiations and was also an opportunity for the pro-Morsi protesters to brace for future attacks. The latter seemed more likely after a speech of Abdel Fattah Sisi, the then Minister of Defense, in late July in which he called upon the Egyptian people to take to the street to show their support for him in his fight against what he called "possible acts of terror." The speech was the alarm that removed any doubt that the military would soon launch attacks against the pro-Morsi protesters in their sit-ins and elsewhere.

It was not a matter of "if" but "when" the military would launch their attack. The pro-MB protesters deployed every skill they learned from January 2011 in standing their ground. The most important lesson was to not leave the square no matter what. Protesters started to set up gates around the Rab'a square, searching those getting in and out of it. Setting up watchdogs and monitoring the media outlets and scanning for the inevitable attack. During the iftar time, protesters would rotate; some would sit to eat and pray while others would be on the lookout watching for any possible military equipment approaching the sit-in to scan for any clues for the zero hour.

Rab'a Massacre

In the few days that followed the end of the holy month of Ramadan, political turbulence was on the rise because the negotiation efforts between the military and anti-Morsi protestors failed. Many of the pro-military media outlets and loyalist journalists were flagrantly advocating for forceful dispersal of the anti-military sit-in. These signals, along with the noticeable increase in security forces in the perimeter of the sit-in, made the sit-in protesters on the tenterhooks as they waited for the military to make a move anytime.

On August 14, 2013, the long-anticipated zero hour was about to break out. That morning, Hussein, who mostly slept in one of the tents close to the field hospital, barely had a chance to get some rest. "We knew it's coming, but we didn't know when—so we were constantly on the lookout," said Hussein. In the early morning, Huessin's older brother woke him up and alerted him that the military was making a move into the sit-in and they should get up and be ready for a long day. "We never planned to use any violence, we just wanted to stand our ground peacefully and practice our right to demonstrate," said Hussein.

No one can confirm with precision when was the first bullet fired, but clashes broke out between the Rab'a protesters and the security forces and escalated very quickly. By 9 a.m., death cases among the protesters were already reported, and Hussein was among the medical team in the field hospital. Most of the wounds and injuries reported to the field hospitals were gunshots in the neck, head, or chest that could only be shot by a skilled marksman or snipers. In his book, David Kirkpatrick (2018), the *New York Times* correspondent in Cairo, stated that "[police] snipers fired down from nearby rooftops. A handful of Islamist protesters near us held up garbage can lid or Styrofoam kickboard to try to shield themselves" (2018, 273).

Human Rights Watch (2014) investigative report that examined the clashes concluded that the police and military forces used excessive and disproportionate lethal force—killing many protesters with direct shots in the head, neck, and chest. The investigation generally estimated between 800–1,000 protesters were killed that day alone. Kirkpatrick (2018) stated that killing of protesters that day was so overwhelming "with no end in sight" (2018, 274).

Every witness I have interviewed on Rab'a, including journalists who attended the sit-in to cover it, said that the violent dispersal was traumatizing, leaving memories that would never be forgotten. An experienced woman journalist who covered the dispersal for an international press outlet shared on her social media page that "when someone mentions the Rab'a dispersal, I suddenly smell blood, regardless of where I am standing at that moment."

Mohamed El Shamy, a photojournalist who covered the Rab'a dispersal for the press described that dispersal as "a massacre." El Shamy, who had much experience covering conflict zones including in South Sudan, Nigeria, and others, described the violent dispersal in Rab'a as more violent than anything he had seen before, "people were falling right and left like birds being shot by snipers."

The events continued to escalate with several protesters reported killed by the police who justified the use of lethal force as a self-defense against the armed pro-Morsi protesters.[15] Two eyewitnesses stated in their interviews that they have seen pistols in the hands of some of the pro-Morsi protesters. The police—the post-dispersal briefing showed videos and photos that documents the presence of a few weapons and ten automatic rifles ("Weapons seized during the dispersal of the Rab'a and al-Nahda sit-ins" 2013). "If the whole group is unarmed, but only one person is armed with a light weapon, that still makes them all dangerous to us," said Major Alaa, a police officer in the riots department. Halem Haneesh, Human Rights Lawyer, disagrees, "even if there is an armed protester, collective punishment to the whole group is not legal or constitutional in any way—the response should always be proportional and targeted." Indeed, there are endless legal and ethical debates on the legitimacy and the efficacy of the use of police violence in group situations when some protesters are using violence, but the majority are not.

Dr. Mostafa, a legal expert on Egypt's criminal law said that, on paper, the Egyptian interim government seem to have followed its legal guidelines. They suspended the constitution but issued a temporary working constitutional declaration then issued a ban on protests without prior approval. At the day of the protest dispersal they broadcasted, via megaphones, that this protest was illegal, and protesters must evict the Rab'a Square immediately and provided safe passages for those who would voluntarily leave the square. However, Dr. Mostafa said the problem was that most of these laws and procedures can easily be contested in an independent court of law for its constitutionality—whether or not the "interim" government is authorized at all to issue such a nationwide ban on a constitutional right like the right to peaceful assembly, especially in the absence of any elected representatives or entities.

And despite these technicalities, legal experts always state that any use of violence by police or military forces should always be limited to the absolute necessities and should be proportional to the threat. Dr. Mostafa said the events like Rab'a dispersal will always be a matter of contestation due to the absence of an independent fact-finding commission that could provide the public with creditable and comprehensive investigation on the events that unfolded that day.

"My brother and I were in Rab'a from day one and none of us had any arms with us—not even a toy gun," Hussein recalled. "That day was nothing but blood, gunshots, and screams." Hussein spent the entire day at the field hospital trying to save lives of fallen and wounded protesters. The field hospital was jampacked beyond capacity and time was passing quickly as everyone in the hospital was trying to do their best to treat as many injured as possible. Hussein was busy, just like everyone else, until one moment when the world stopped spinning for him when the newest patient that entered the hospital was a familiar face. "It was my brother laying on the stretcher with blood covering his chest. He had no pulse." His older brother suffered two 9mm bullets in his left-side chest which led to his death by the time he arrived at the field hospital.

"I couldn't take his lack of response as an answer."

"I performed every medical procedure I knew or learnt or read about to save his life—no luck."

"I called every doctor in the hospital to help—no luck."

Hussein was very close to his older brother who paid for most of his tuition fees for medical school, helped him through tough times in school, and used to hang out together when school exams overwhelmed him.

"He was my role model, my mentor, he was everything you want to have in an older brother."

As devastated as he was, he insisted on continuing his work at the field hospital. The lack of doctors and the overwhelming count of injuries didn't leave a chance for him to grieve the loss of his brother. He took a moment to pray for his brother and tried to reach his second brother, who was also in the protest, but could not locate him at this moment.

In a short and intense interview on Aljazeera Channels, the director of the field hospital stated that they had received more than seven hundred cases—including two hundred shot with live ammunition in less than three hours ("In Charge of the Field Hospital in Rab'a Al-Adawiya" 2013). Hussein said that what started as "treating wounds" quickly turned to "counting dead bodies."

The police and military were winning ground and clearing the protest in a steady feat and were inching their way toward the field hospital. "We knew we are losing this battle but assumed that they would at least respect the medical team and the dead bodies—but we were wrong." When the police stormed the hospital, they were running around breaking shelves, spilling medicine jars on the ground, and randomly arresting whoever they could. Videos shot by independent bloggers show a military-operated earthmover clearing the street where dead bodies were resting on the curbside without any regard to the cultural sacredness of respecting the dead ("A bulldozer bulldozes dozens of the bodies of the victims of the fourth massacre" 2013).

Medical staff started running out of the hospital to avoid being arrested; after all they couldn't do their job any more after the police destroyed their hospital. Hussein lost track of his colleagues but went to look for what had been declared as "safe passage"; a passage that should have given protesters a safe exit to the outer street except that it didn't. Police, military, and undercover agents were on the hunt and Hussein was among those captured.

Hussein, along with dozens of other protesters were shoveled into a big police vehicle. They didn't know what their destination was, but they knew it would not be a place they would like to be. The vehicles were dark, reeking, jampacked, and so hot that no one could lean on its inside shell. Temperature registered in Cairo that day was high—93F/33C—which of course would be a lot hotter inside a poorly ventilated steel vehicle with a total of four 13 in. × 13 in. rusty grilled windows that can barely let any air in or out.

There was no place for Hussein to sit on the bench inside the vehicle. Benches were given for elderly people and those with bad wounds and injuries. In the vehicle, Hussein met a familiar face, a friend of his younger brother who approached Hussein and petted his shoulder in mourning for the loss of his brother. He told Hussein "he was a great friend and will always be remembered" to which Hussein nodded to in agreement before he paused for a second. That was his younger brother's friend, not the older brother.

"Who are you talking about?" Hussein asked in distress.

"Your brother, Mahmoud," he answered.

This is when Hussein realized that he had just lost both his brothers in the dispersal, not just the older brother!

Meanwhile, Saeed, who was also volunteering in a Rab'a field hospital had just heard his share of bad news. His older brother, Aly, was just shot and was pronounced dead. Aly, unlike Saeed, was not religious at all. "You could easily confuse him with a famous movie star," said a friend of Saeed. Both brothers were very close, and Aly's death was devastating.

Unlike Hussein, Saeed was lucky enough not to be arrested the day of the sit-in dispersal. Somehow, he was able to flee the scene. Saeed planned to document and publish what happened with his brother in order to seek accountability. The following months would see Saeed organizing peaceful rallies and demonstrations raising banners and posters demanding justice for his brother and seeking the bare minimum of holding those who killed his unarmed brother accountable.

Meanwhile, Hussein was locked with other inmates in a detention facility and frequently interrogated by National Security police officers. Several torture techniques were used with Hussein that varied from beating, sleep deprivation, and electrocuting in sensitive body parts including his genitalia.

After approximately two months of torture and interrogation that ended with Hussein being forced to appear in a video to confess and declare responsibility for acts of violence that he says he never committed. He was transferred to a prosecutor, with a forged arrest date, forged confession, and a list of sham charges. Although Hussein managed to meet an attorney after a few months, he never met him again, because that attorney was himself arrested a few weeks later, on accusations of "inciting violent mobilization" and "cooperating with an outlawed organization."

Prison, Hussein says, was better than the detention facility as the beating and physical torture was less frequent, if compared with the National Security's controlled detention centers. But he lived with his agony that deepened every day. The arrest of his lawyer, Hussein says, was his last hope for pursuit of any justice through legal means. "It was the stroke that broke the camel's back," said Hussein who, after losing hope of any justice, would actively seek more radical means of retaliation against the state.

In his pursuit to campaign for his brother, Saeed sought the help of his Muslim Brotherhood *Osra* (translates as family). *Osra* is the first building block in the greater formation of the Muslim Brotherhood. Every member of the brotherhood belongs to an *Osra* through which they receive religious education and mentorship by more senior members (naqeeb). The mentorship extends beyond religious doctrine to several aspects of life including personal skills, carrying out community and social activities together. Mentors are responsible for establishing a relationship with the members of the group, befriending them, guiding them through life events, and encouraging cohesion and solidarity among members of *Osra* as well as between the *Osra* and the Brotherhood writ large.

A Muslim Brotherhood member explains that the relationship between a mentor and Osra members is extremely important. A mentor is a figure and role model, you trust them with your secrets, learn from them, and they basically become an older brother to you. In turn, some mentors see the MB youth as their young brothers, or even sometimes children. Saeed's Osra and its mentor provided him with substantial help in organizing multiple rallies, demonstrations, and marches that denounced the military coup and called for justices to the victims of Rab'aa sit-in and freeing political detainees.

One day, as Saeed and his colleagues were marching with their banners and posters and chanting with the same demands that they had been circulating for months, a police force ambushed them. As the protesters tried to escape, the police shot and killed some of them including a fifteen-year-old child.

"This incident was devastating for everyone who knew the child," said a person who had known Saeed very well. This was a turning point for Saeed and his close friends from that *Osra*. It was after the death of one of their close friends in the demonstration that Saeed decided that violence was their only way to fight the state.

In the meantime, after several months of imprisonment, Hussein was transferred to see the prosecutor who routinely renewed his detention. But this time the prosecutor decided to release Hussein and several others pending their investigation. "I don't know why I was arrested, and I have no idea why I was released," said Hussein.

The brutality of the Rab'a massacre and its ripple effects left a huge impact on many people. It didn't matter whether you were a protester, a journalist, a doctor, or even an onlooker, the bloodbath left a scar that would live with everyone—perhaps forever.

When Hussein was released, he was fixated on just one objective; to do every possible thing to take justice in his own hand—even if that meant taking up arms and fighting those who wrecked his life and killed his two brothers while peacefully protesting the military coup.

TAREK

The third story takes us to Upper Egypt. It is technically the south of Egypt but the higher elevation of its land that allows the Nile River to flow northbound toward the capital and on to its main branches that end in the Mediterranean. This land is named "Upper Egypt." It is rich with fertile soil, natural resources, and, most importantly, it is home to a vast amount of ancient Egyptian monuments which makes it a unique part of Egypt.

Yet despite its economic potential and historical significance, the south has suffered from decades of governmental apathy and institutional negligence which eventually made it home to the poorest five cities in Egypt with an average of 51.9 percent of its population under the national poverty line (El Sayed 2019). Lack of services, infrastructure, and job opportunities made the life of an average person very challenging—and pushed youth to migrate, either to Cairo or to outside of Egypt looking for better life opportunities.

Tarek, a twenty-two-year-old man, grew up in one of the poorest cities in Egypt's south. But unlike many of his friends, he made an early choice to stay in his town to help his aging parents maintain their small farmland, the family's main source of income. But that was not the only reason he wanted to stay in the village. Tarek said that despite the financial hardships, the village was his home. He loved the neighbors, the culture, their family's small farmland and he simply did not feel the urge to leave.

Upper Egypt has distinct cultural and social characteristics. Family, kinship, and traditions play a key role in shaping the public conscious and social relations. It is indeed more socially conservative than the lower (northern) side of Egypt or the urban coastal cities. And just like many traditionalist families in Egypt, cousin marriage is one of the most common ways to get married, especially in this region where cultural conservativism and gender segregation makes it challenging for relationships to be established independently. Tarek didn't challenge this social pattern, he was already in love with his cousin, Manal, and their whole family was endorsing this bond.

Due to their family relation, arranging the marriage was simple and smooth. The only problematic issue the couple faced was the timing of their wedding; there was a rush from one side to get the couple married so that their aging grandmother could attend and bless their eternal bond, but on the other hand Manal had to first complete her undergraduate degree before any arrangement for wedding would take place.

The couple and their parents were excited and couldn't be happier seeing their beloved children growing up and getting together. Tarek worked tirelessly to save as much money as he possibly could in order to build and perfect their future home. He leaned on his friends' skills and time to help him paint in an effort to cut some costs.

Everything seemed normal and their life was progressing, despite the grave political changes in Egypt, until one day, in early 2014, when Manal took part in a pro-Morsi demonstration in an avenue that is nearby her home. Although not all her siblings were active members of the Muslim Brotherhood, Manal's parents were active and were used to taking part in many of the Brotherhood activities. Manal herself was not very active, but she used to be an occasional participant in some events, especially the social ones that had more to do with charity and social festivities than politics. Not that she didn't believe in the group's cause or political positions, but she was critical of the group's lack of gender equality, especially that women were not taking senior positions inside the group.

Women members of the Muslim Brotherhood or "the sisters" were traditionally limited to social work, charitable activities, and other supportive tasks, rather than primary political roles inside the group or in public life (Allam 2012; Abdel Moneim 2011; Tamam 2013). The MB leadership usually justified a limited role for women members in Egypt's political life as a protective measure to women from the authoritarian ruling regimes that would do harm to women so men put themselves in the forefront lines to spare women this humiliation (Allam 2012).

Sarah,[16] a former member of the MB, said in an interview for this book that "It doesn't matter how educated, well-spoken, or brave a woman is, male leaders were the ones to make the final decisions—even if women were consulted on some matters, it was just a facade." Many women struggled against such a discriminatory policy that had been established many years ago. There were some successes and failures over time but the "January 25 uprising was an opportunity to rebel against these norms," said Sarah who like many other women have tried to benefit from the general atmosphere in 2011 to push for larger roles for women inside the group and in public life, especially as the uprising was imposing new realities.

Indeed, the Muslim Brotherhood showed flexibility under strong social pressure. In 2012, women members of the MB were allowed, for the first time, to run for positions like heads of regional women committees; a position that despite its obvious meaning to women, was solely held by men. In the following months, the Muslim Brotherhood would push more women into different senior positions in the government, the president's office, parliament, as well as in several committees of the Muslim Brotherhood newly established political party: Freedom and Justice Party (FJP).

But Sarah, who was deeply involved in the civic work of the group, thinks that these moves were merely a political maneuver rather than a reflection of progressive change in the group's policies. She cites an incident with Khairt El Shater, one of the most influential figures of the Muslim Brotherhood and was the group's first candidate for the 2012 presidential elections before he got disqualified by the elections commission. El Shater called for a meeting in his office where he was trying to build a team of young MB recruits to be tasked with attending international conferences and make media appearances to enhance the groups' image and help reach out to the newer audience.

Sarah, who was among the attendees of that meeting, showed interest in being part of this new team. But El Shater was concerned that Sarah, alone, should not travel to international conferences; he asserted she must have a male guardian with her, or else she won't be able to travel.

"It was façade of progressiveness, but they didn't believe that women are equal to men," said Sarah who will shortly after this meeting split away from the Muslim Brotherhood although her family remains faithful members of the group to this day.

But the women members of the group dealt with some extraordinary challenges in the aftermath of the military coup in 2013. When the crackdown started on the Muslim Brotherhood, whether at sit-ins or at their homes, hundreds of leaders (who are predominantly men) were identified as targets of state security. As the situation worsened, particularly with more male leadership being arrested, killed, or disappeared every day, women assumed *de facto* leadership of what was left of the group, not just to advocate for the rights of the detainees but also to fight against the country's new dictators.

Manal was one of those who found herself in a position to play a critical role to mobilize for anti-military protests. "She would write the banners herself, arrange the rally routes, coordinate with other protesters in the area, and plan emergency escape routes herself," said Tarek. One day,[17] Manal informed her fiancée of her plan to take part in one of the protests which was planned to take about two hours—nothing out of the ordinary, she had done that several times before. But unlike prior protests, this rally was ambushed and attacked by plain-clothed individuals—which are in most cases either undercover police, or informants for the police. When the attack took place, some women participants ran to adjacent alleyways to seek shield from the police—they had faced this aggression before and escaping to different streets saved them in the past, but not this time.

The police harassment, this time, did not stop by dispersing the rally or beating the protesters up, the chase led to the arrest of several participants, including Manal.

The news of Manal's arrest reached Tarek, who ran in every direction trying to locate her whereabouts. The police initially denied that she was in their custody but after awhile, they were able to pinpoint her location through a well-connected family friend who was able to find her. She was detained in a nearby Central Security Facility which was temporarily set up as an overflow prison.

The slight relief they felt when they located her quickly subsided when they heard Manal's shocking testimony before the district prosecutor. Manal claimed that she had been sexually assaulted while handcuffed and blindfolded by police personnel. Her lawyer requested an investigation into this incident, but the prosecution ignored the incident and never charged any of the officers who had held Manal in custody at the time, and only focused on charging her with the prefabricated charges of "joining a terrorist organization," "destabilizing the social peace," etc.

"Who would she terrorize? She is an angel," said Tarek, who emphasized that it had taken him a great deal of courage to talk about his fiancé's sexual assault incident.

Manal's assault was not a rare event, especially in the period between 2013 and 2014. Multiple independent investigations have documented the accounts of several women who were sexually assaulted, harassed inside police stations, prisoner-transfer vehicles or in other unidentified locations while in police custody (Aman 2014).

One notable case was that of Tasneem, a female detainee who was released in late 2013, and who later described her arrest events to *Al-Monitor*. She stated that several security agents chased her and grabbed her by her clothes and dragged her all the way into a police vehicle where an officer hit her with a baton on sensitive body parts. Tasneem said that when she stepped into the car, there was another female detainee who was bleeding and had scratch marks on her face. The detainee told Tasneem that officers were demeaning her and other female students, saying, "They threatened to rape me and the other girls" (Hamed 2014).

Anas Altikriti, founder and CEO of the Cordoba Foundation in London, and human rights lawyer Islam Salameh confirmed in an investigative report that raping female prisoners is becoming a systematic practice inside Egypt's detention facilities. They both confirmed that they have received evidence and testimony regarding cases of rape in detention centers that occurred at the hands of officers and agents of the police force (Hamed 2014). Mustafa al-Hadda, another human rights activist, also confirmed that "the incumbent regime has allegedly adopted the abuse as a policy against opponents of the government. The policy is to humiliate, traumatize and to render them politically impotent," al-Hadda said (*Al Jazeera News* April 1, 2014).

And while sexuality in Egypt is considered one of many taboo topics, sex in a conservative culture like Upper Egypt is a whole other level. Talking about or engaging in sexual activities outside the frame of marriage is not socially permitted. Moreover, the female's body represents honor for the whole family. A man's honor is dependent and tied to the purity (sexual virginity) of his female family members.

Any engagement of sexual activity, outside the frame of marriage, is considered a direct assault on the family's honors and thus, men—as guardians of this honor, are expected to take action to counter any assault on their female family members in an attempt to "clean away the shame" which explains, to some extent, the strong presence of honor crimes in Egypt.

Honor killing and honor crimes are very common in Egypt. In fact, the National Center for Social and Criminal Studies (2016) reported that 92 percent of violence against women including murder cases were motivated by issues of "honor." Moreover, the legal system is greatly influenced by the cultural component in the sense that it does favor men, by either punishing them less or not at all in cases of honor crimes, reported Rabab Abdo in an interview with the press.

And while Tarek and Manal did not commit an honor crime in the cultural sense, the sexual assault on Manal had a similar effect on Tarek's family honor. The difference here is that Manal was recognized by her family as a victim rather than a partner in this "honor wrongdoing."

Tarek recounts the moments he knew about the police's involvement in sexually assaulting his fiancé by saying "it was as if you set me ablaze." He was furious, hurt, and outraged. The family lawyer took additional steps in trying to file an official complaint in both the ministry of interior inspection department as well as suing the minister of interior to force him to take an action with respect of the sexual assault allegation, but three months passed without any progress. Manal is still in state custody, her case is pending, and all her complaints on sexual assault went unnoticed. Meanwhile Tarek's frustration was steadily increasing, "I was boiling with every single day," said Tarek who alleged that he had consumed all possible means to hold those responsible accountable, without any luck.

In late 2014, Tarek, for the first time, got a chance to visit Manal in prison. This was the first time they met since her arrest. The visitation time was limited, but Tarek described it as worse than anything he had ever experienced, especially when she told him about her assault and the humiliation she had experienced by the different police personnel.

The visitation, Tarek recalls was not like anything he imagined, "she was ruins of a human," he stated. "She was broken, defeated, and damaged," added

Tarek who said seeing his fiancée assaulted and humiliated—let alone wrong-fully arrested for the mere fact of peacefully protesting, was beyond bearable.

Tarek explained that he couldn't stand still, watching his fiancé being humiliated and assaulted in complete absence of any chance to save her. Especially that he was also under societal pressure from his and Manal's family—who expected him to act in ways that restore the family's honor. Within a few days of the visitation, Tarek would be in touch with friends from his hometown who would help him take the measures he perceived as "fair and justified" to avenge his fiancé—even if that meant he would take up arms.

NOTES

1. Locations and means of communication with interviewees will remain undisclosed.

2. Actual location of the interview or means of communication will remain undisclosed to protect identity of the interviewees, their families, and their friends.

3. During a state of emergency in Egypt, citizens' constitutional rights are suspended, police authorities are increased, and remains are mostly unchecked by judiciary. Police can, and could, use the state of emergency as pretext to eliminate political mobilization, street protests, rights of association, freedom of speech, and detain, with lax limits, any citizen that they presume dangerous.

4. Studies vary on the exact space of the square, but they vary from 30k sq. m which is (322k sq. ft) to 50k sq. m which is (538k sq. ft).

5. Name changed.

6. Khiary Ramadan speaks at CBC. https://www.youtube.com/watch?v=ubgdoUjgbNg.

7. Ahmed Moussa interview on Sada El Blad TV. https://www.youtube.com/watch?v=2bG8zghmi4c.

8. Lamees Al Hadidi speaking on multiple channels. https://www.youtube.com/watch?v=MMa7149g_L4.

9. Name changed.

10. Name changed.

11. A proverb that means "disappearing."

12. Essam Sultan video to the court. https://www.youtube.com/watch?v=x1ME5xmZ74Y.

13. Essam Al Arian video statement (2016). Via *Al Watan News*. https://www.youtube.com/watch?v=l_cCVcpO8Eo.

14. There is no credible empirical data that estimates the volume of support that either side have ever received without being tinted with a political favoritism.

15. Egypt's Ministry of Interior Press Conference 2013. http://gate.ahram.org.eg/News/383155.aspx.

16. Name changed.

17. Date undisclosed for identity protection.

Chapter Two

Extremism Is in
the Eye of the Beholder

Three different individuals; Ramy, Hussein, and Tarek. Each with their own grievance, perceptions, moral paradigms, emotional and societal pressures that would all come together in what almost looks like a combustion chamber to spark the trigger of violence cycle in their life. Each one of them thought taking up arms was the right action to settle their grievance through waging a war against their adversaries in the form of state institutions and their representative personnel. Institutions like military, police, prosecution, judiciary, and other state affiliated officials and public figures were considered legitimate targets to their attacks.

Stories of Ramy, Hussein, Tarek and others show the complexity and intricacy of such transformative process and its underlying dynamics. Answering questions about why, how, and under what conditions do individuals or groups transform from nonviolent activism to violent insurgency is, accordingly, anything but straightforward. In this study I pay a special attention to the individual experiences rather than just the macro influences that has been traditionally the focus of the scholarship. Emotions, aspirations, trauma, as well as other sociocultural and political factors are all carefully examined and assessed.

But before I attempt to offer possible answers, it is important to set clear the definitions and terminologies. In particular what I mean when I refer to "violent radicalization" or "violent extremism" or "terrorism" and the ilk.

The term *terrorism* and its theoretical and political trajectories are extremely ambiguous due to the large number of discussions and debates that float around them, making the term so fungible that it is rendered meaningless. It references almost any and all types of political opponents, depending on the political regime in question—whether globally or locally. The lack of a viable and unequivocal grand theory of radical violent extremism/terrorism makes any definition of the term incapable of accurately reflecting the political commitments and stakes involved, since the term is stretched to include a broad grouping of heterogeneous political and militant acts and actors under a single label. It is more oriented to enabling a range of political and regulatory measures of security nature rather than the solid challenge it actually faces.

Moreover, the term *terrorism* has traditionally been conflated with other terms like "*violent extremism,*" "*radicalism,*" and "*insurgency.*" And since there is no clear or unified definition of any these terms, they have been used interchangeably to describe various groups of different degrees of violent aspirations (sometimes even groups of no violence affiliations at all). This lack of clarity and constant swap of terms opens the door for the term to be politically appropriated, especially by government agencies, to designate select groups, as violent/extremist/terrorist. The basis of the designation is more often than not motivated by security concerns (whether national security or just mere political regime stability, especially in autocratic regimes), to accuse their political opponents of being terrorists to ultimately isolate or eliminate their role as a political rival.

THE DEFINITION—JACKING

Not only are these definitions ambiguous and misleading, but they are also greatly influenced by political biases and ideological favoritism. What constitutes a *terrorist* to the government of Egypt for example, is not the same in Saudi Arabia, Jordan, or Morocco and so on. Although these Arab States are culturally, politically, and geographically close to each other, their understanding of radical violent extremism/terrorism is built on their own national security priorities, not on an impartial examination of the phenomenon. The variations in national security priorities between countries thus breeds different definitions and classifications.

Besides, the term is regularly used by politicians and experts to tailor accusations against their global and regional rivals, ideological competitors, or even domestic political dissidents. Egypt's designation of the Muslim Brotherhood as a terrorist organization is for example, primarily motivated by domestic political rivalry to the setting president rather than a thorough examination of the group's behavior or their root causes of violence. In fact, some scholars argue that such a politically motivated designation could push a nonviolent group underground and encourage its members to turn to violence since they have nothing to lose—and are accused of violence anyway (Kurtz and Smithey 2008).

Turk (2002c) argues that the politicizing definitions and terminologies like *radical violent extremism/terrorism* is a normal practice in any ideological warfare between a state and its opponents. The stronger party often gets the chance to define what constitutes radical violent extremism/terrorism, and selectively apply it on their enemy. Politics, not independent rationale, is what usually defines the terrorist.

In fact, this dilemma is not unique to autocratic regimes. Even in well-established democracies, government agencies still struggle to come up with one understanding, let alone a single definition, of terrorism. Security services, intelligence agencies, and law enforcement have some working definitions for *terrorism* that do not necessarily conform with any paradigm other than their own, sometimes eccentric, perception of the phenomenon at a given time—but not necessarily based on a scholastic or well-researched model. The United Kingdom's home office looks at *radical violent extremism* separately from *terrorism* and defines it as "the process by which a person comes to support terrorism and extremist ideologies associated with terrorist groups." Almost every word of this definition could be debated and broke down into many different—even contradicting—meanings.

The convoluted nature of *terrorism*, which combines challenges that vary from security, society, economy, and politics, as well as distinctive cultural paradigms, makes it almost impossible to tackle or address as a single homogenous question. Instead, those with most resources and authority, often the government security agencies and their affiliate entities, get to dominate how we see and understand this process. This is what I see as a "definition-jacking" process that limits not only how a society sees the problem, but also shapes the efforts of response to them.

And as the world advances over time, so does our understanding of social phenomena. One of the early explanations of terrorism was put forward by Le Bon (1916, 391) in his study of the psychology of collective behavior where he argued that violence can be perpetuated by anti-government revolutionaries as "means to impress their enemies" and influence the political power— he called that act "terrorism." But since then, different theories, paradigms, definitions, have evolved to elucidate different aspects of the term—all based on new world events and the ever-changing political circumstances at a given time.

But as definition grew wider to meet different global challenges and satisfy various political powers, the term *"terrorism"* lost its integrity and became obsolete—it almost referred to everything and nothing at the same time. In addition to being ethically contested and politically loaded. So gradually some scholars and experts started to put forward the term *"violent extremism"* as an attempt to bypass the confusion that is associated with the term *"terrorism,"* but also to restore some integrity in the designation.

Violent extremism as an improved term was only moderately successful—because again it is used interchangeably with *terrorism* and other similar terms without clear guidelines. Furthermore, the very word *"extremism"* poses another challenge in and of its own. The word "extreme" presumes a sharp departure from the "norm" which opens the door to question who decides what is the *norm*? Those who determine the norm—in any setting—get to rule what is the extreme. But since such a central authority doesn't exist, this assumption remains subjective to each individual. In other words, do extremists see themselves as extremists? Fighters of the Islamic State (ISIL, ISIS), who are seen by millions of people as extremists, see themselves as representatives of the righteous—normal—form of Islam while seeing the modern society as "deviant" from the norm." Extremism is in the eye of the beholder.

This is not to mention that yesterday's norm is not tomorrow's norm, which subsequently means that what we see today as extremism doesn't necessary mean it's going to remain the extremism of tomorrow. There was some time in recent history when slavery or killing of native populations was considered the norm and was socially accepted. On the contrary today, a society that doesn't guarantee equal rights to all its citizens despite their color, sex, place of origin, etcetera is seen as an extremist society.

Another popular term that is often thrown into the same ever-melting pot of definitions is the term *"radicalization."* And while that term could be seen as slightly different than the above terms because it mainly refers to a "process," it still has its share of murkiness.

Borum (2011a, 9, 12) defines radicalization as "the process of developing extremist ideologies and beliefs." Crossett and Spitaletta suggest a broader understanding "the process by which an individual, group, or mass of people undergo a transformation participating in the political process via legal means to the use or support of violence for political purposes."

But does just having some sort of *extremist* thought enough to make someone a violent person? Some scholars, like Peter Neumann (2015), Shaban (2015), and Zidan (2009) struggle to distance the radical thinking from the radical action. Neumann (2015) notes that the "principal conceptual fault-line is between notions of radicalization that emphasize extremist beliefs ('cognitive radicalization'), and those that focus on extremist behavior ('behavioral radicalization')." The scholarship, despite its efforts to define the phenomenon, failed to clarify whether cognitive radicalization (radical thinking) is a *sine qua non* to radical violent action or not.

The complexity of definitions and terminologies makes it very challenging for academics and professionals alike to focus their efforts on what matters, which is examining and understanding how and why people turn to deadly tactics of violence especially in collective settings. The phenomenon is complex enough and doesn't call for additional complications or hurdles. It is as if we are running in our place—fighting unwarranted battles and achieving very little while violent groups make significant leaps in their tactics, strategies, and recruitment methods.

However, of all terms above, I opt to use "violent radicalization" as it is, comparatively, the most explanatory term that fits the case of this book the most. I also define the term *violent radicalization* as "the process in which individuals abandon their nonviolent commitments and switch to violent tactics in the course of their political engagement with the state."

It is very important to emphasize that this book is not intended and does not attempt to issue moral judgments on any individual or group that are part of this discussion or in any part of this research. For this reason, I will avoid deploying any propagative vocabulary when describing any groups or individuals in this study. Instead of using *terrorism/violent extremism*, I elect to use rather a simple, unadorned, term that just describes the nature of the group in question: violent insurgents. Additionally, I will give this term only to groups who openly and willingly declare the usage of violence as part of their tactics.

Scholarship on Violent Radicalization

Existing literature offers ample theoretical explanations to human behavioral transformation, whether individually or in a form of collective action. Different approaches are, however, emblematic of the specifics of social science branches they come from. Some disciplines are deeply invested in clinical experiments, others rely on data quantifications, but none have produced any grand theories that suggest a fixed course of radicalization. Instead, scholars identified a number of motivating factors that either work independently or together to prompt people to choose violence.

These motivating factors varied from religion (Zidan 2009; Huntington 1993), or the lack of thereof (Juergensmeyer 2003; Emerson and Hartman 2004), political repression (Pape 2005; Turk 2004; Hafez 2004; Iannaccone 1997), social exclusion (Turk 2004; Iannaccone 1997), and economic distress and social injustices (Collins 1975). Some scholars like Crenshaw (1981) even argue that turning to violence is effective for many social movements because it is louder and flashier in voicing their protest.

Whether based on empirical data or merely driven by abstract philosophies, there are some well-founded theories that explain violent radicalization. Each has its own merits, reasoning, and rationale that support their existence. Many of these theories, however, fall short of offering a plausible explanation to the current wave of violent radicalization in Egypt in the era following the 2011 mass uprising. For instance, theories that focused on questioning the mental and psychological status of the individuals who engage in mass violence implying that only "deviant psychopaths" can become violent individuals in such a manner (Borum 2011b) are misplaced. Such theories received very limited evidence to back their proposition (Atran 2003; Sageman 2004; McCauley and Moskalenko 2011). Sageman's (2004, 83) extensive study on Al-Qaeda for example, concluded that "*terrorists* are surprisingly normal in their mental health." Besides, such a clinical approach, even if pertinent in some cases, ignores the sociocultural contexts, political atmosphere, and ideological motivations that could contribute, significantly, to the violent radicalization of individuals.

And while at the outset of my inquiry, I was not ruling out any possible causes, I did not observe any obvious mental disorders or behavioral abnormalities in either Ramy's behavior or any of the other interviewees. Thus, I had to go beyond the clinical—also classical—approach and look for further, more plausible, explanations.

Instead of demonstrating all theories in one or two chapters—just to conclude that they do not work—I will choose a different approach where only relevant theories will be examined apropos of the Egyptian case. To do so I will start by presenting the Egyptian government's line of rationalization. In other words, what is Egypt's government accusing these activists of and why did they think they were turning into violence? Then, I will test their narrative against the relevant theories and compare them to the data collected for this study.

The Egyptian Government's Side of the Story

Aly,[1] a police officer interviewed for this book on conditions of anonymity explained that after the military had ousted President Mohamed Morsi, law enforcement agencies were bracing for a potential backlash from Morsi's supporters. He added that there was a common understanding among police officers based on some intel received from state agencies that the Muslim Brotherhood and their Islamist allies won't let go of governance easily and that the Muslim Brotherhood were expected to use violence against military and police forces to reinstate Mohamed Morsi as president.

"So, we had to be prepared and carry out some preemptive ops," said the officer whose testimony comes in line with the interim government's discourse that warned the public against the "potential terrorism." And while there was no formal definition or explanation to what constitutes "potential terrorism," the measures taken by the government revealed much of the government's vision and targets.

The prophecy of violent attacks on police and military appeared to be right. The months that followed the ouster of President Mohamed Morsi did witness an influx of violent confrontations and attacks on multiple governmental facilities and public officials. The government categorically attributed all these attacks to the Muslim Brotherhood members who, the government claimed, were ready to do anything to stay in power, including using violent means (see Egypt's MFA, Nabil Fahmy's speech at the UNGA 2014; Fahim 2013).

In late 2013, the Egyptian government designated the Muslim Brotherhood a terrorist organization, banned all its activities, and seized its assets. In its declaration, the Egyptian government cited the Muslim Brotherhood's history of violence and assassinations and stated that the government won't allow these acts to reoccur in modern-day Egypt. Military loyalist figures and media pundits followed suit and used their platform to blast the Muslim Brotherhood and blame them for all attacks, even if other unrelated groups have declared their responsibility. For example, on December 24, 2013—one day before the government had designed the MB as a terrorist organization—an attack took place on Mansoura's Police Directorate (North of Cairo) leaving more than fourteen police officers killed and many others injured (Al Ahram 2013c). Within a few hours, the government attributed the attack to the Muslim Brotherhood and promised further actions against the group. But much to everybody's surprise, a group (who fundamentally criticized the Muslim Brotherhood for multiple reasons) under the name Ansar Bait Al Makdas (currently Sinai Province), declared responsibility for the attack (Fahim and El Sheikh 2013). This is one example where the government preferred to allocate blame on the group—without any transparent or credible investigation or disclosing any evidence—to designate the group as a terrorist organization, demonstrating how abruptly such critical conclusions are drawn.

This was not to exonerate the Muslim Brotherhood from wrongdoing, but to say that examples like the above, which lack transparency and independent investigation, make it almost impossible to rely on the government claims as a reliable source of information. But the government continued to relentlessly exploit this claim not just domestically, but also internationally (see Nabil Fahmy's speech at the UNGA 2014) and have advocated for the designation of the Muslim Brotherhood as a terrorist organization, internationally.

The government has also used the violent history of the Muslim Brother-hood together with the group's religious background to frame the conflict as "modern government versus religious fundamentalist groups." Officer Aly stated that "the young members of the Muslim Brotherhood who are involved in violent attacks are influenced by hardline clerics in the group who exploited the youth's dire economic situation and lack of proper education and fueled them into violent confrontation with the state."

This line of argumentation [religious fundamentalism as motivation] has materialized in President Abdel Fattah El Sisi's speeches who appeared on multiple occasions to make the case for the role of fundamentalism in motivating political violence in Egypt. In a nutshell, he argued that there was an outdated and misinterpreted form of Islam that had been circulating over the past decades and had been continuously used by religious fanatics including those of the Muslim Brotherhood to recruit new calibers. In his speech in Davos Forum 2015, the president stated that "the terrible terrorist attacks and this terrible image of Muslims led us to think that we must stop and think and change the religious discourse and remove from it the things that have led to violence and extremism." The president had also called for what he named a "religious revolution" to appropriate the religious discourse and filter it from fanatical ideas. This narrative became the party line adopted by most local press outlets, media, state institutions including the religious entities. Calls for religious discourse reforms swept the nation as the regime propagators circulated their support to such a demand.

Gradually this rationalization turned into a deliberate and methodical effort to associate "terrorism" in Egypt with religious fundamentalism (or rather an outdated form and interpretation of Islam). Indeed, the largest share of blame fell on the shoulders of the Muslim Brotherhood whose leadership was depicted by the government—according to the collected and analyzed data—as the fanatics who exploited the youth's economic and social vulnerabilities to push them into committing acts of mass violence. And whether the Brotherhood has been truly involved, and indeed used religious discourse to motive its youth—and other youth—to commit acts of violence is something that will be addressed in later a stage of this book. But before we get there, it is important to first examine whether religion, alone, can be a driver behind violent radicalization in general, and in Egypt in particular, as claimed by the government of Egypt.

Is Religion the Right Answer?

Testing the government of Egypt's theory is not an easy mission. After all, the Middle East is a place where religion constitute an integral part of the configuration of the public consciousness (Amin 2005). And thus, the involvement of religious ideas, beliefs, and traditions in everyday routines is standard. But how far these religious rituals and beliefs could have affected the behavior of Egyptian youth in committing violence in Egypt post-2011 is the question.

Religion—or to be more specific, religious fundamentalism—as motivation of violence is perhaps one of the most common and popular explanations to violent radicalization. The aftermath of the 9/11 attacks and the waves of religion-framed violence that followed it, predisposed both the international community and local populations to accept religion as a powerful trigger that, alone, could motivate individuals to commit severe acts of violence against other groups that don't share the same religious beliefs. Numerous theories have been developed over the years to argue and demonstrate just that. Hence, relating religion to violence became tempting, and sometimes even an easy answer, especially when one of the government key opponents is a religion-based movement that had historically incubated some of the most influential figures of religious fundamentalism like Sayyed Qutub, Abdallah Azzam, Ayman El Zawahry, and others.

The significance of religion, as a force behind violent radicalization, lays in its ability to act as an ideological powerhouse that supplies its devotees with divine approval, endorsement, and sometimes even an obligation to act in a certain manner. Islam is especially significant in this sense because it doesn't have a central authority or a unified command to approve or disapprove one single interpretation of pious orders. Despite the strict rules set forth by historic Muslim scholars, it all boils down to every individual's own understanding of the godly orders. The Qur'an—the main source of guidance and legislation in Islam—though written in Arabic is not an easy text to read and understand even for native Arabic speakers. Interpreting the Qur'an requires assistance from scholars who help not only explain the meaning of the difficult vocabulary, verses, and teachings, but also tie these verses to other rituals and traditions, especially the prophet's teachings and sayings, in order to be able to make sense of it all. This level of difficulty, and somehow inaccessibility, together with the absence of sacerdotal order or a command structure, while theoretically eliminating religious authority, it does open the door for multiple different models and interpretations; each with its own principals, values, beliefs, and philosophy—and thus, its own ideology.

As Islam has different interpretations, so does its political ideology. There are assorted versions, definitions, and interpretations of the political project of Islam that vary from one group to another. In its core, political Islam may advocate that public, social, and political life should follow the provisions of the Islamic Sharia. But the interpretation of this project, once again, varies greatly from one group to another. From the nonviolent Sufi groups to the most violent, like the Islamic State (ISIL) and Al-Qaeda. Each group claims that they represent the purest and righteous form of Islam and its political project.

The varying interpretation are not just on the face concept of "political Islam" but even offspring versions such as Salafi Jihadism. Groups like Al-Gama'a al-Islamiyya of Egypt, Al Qaeda, Algerian Armed Islamic Group, Islamic State, and Al-Nusra Front, among others, have claimed to embrace one form or another of Salafi Jihadism, albeit with different strategic priorities and some interpretational divergences.

Salafism is Sunni Muslim doctrine that could be seen as a fresher account of Wahhabism that originated in the eighteenth century in response to the influences of modernization and westernization that Muslim societies experienced during the age of colonialism. The principal idea was to study the first three generations of Muslims who lived with, or immediately after, the Prophet Muhammed, and revive this era in all its aspects because it was the golden era of Islam and its birth. These three generations, who witnessed glorious days, represent the untainted pre-modern form of Islam that all Muslims should look to and learn from. That entails the rejection of new practices that the prophet and his companions did not personally carry, stricter enforcement of Sharia laws, and a conservative literalist interpretation of Qur'an, among others.

Salafi Jihadism is one form of ideology that allows use of physical force to ensure the compliance with Islamic Sharia law, including the use of force against perceived enemies. This enemy could be anything from local government (and its institutions, representatives, and allies), foreign military and police, political parties, other religious groups. It has been the foundational ideological ground for many violent Islamist groups over the years and is still just as powerful today.

Could that be the answer: Salafi Jihadism is what motivates modern-day violent radicalization in Egypt?

Well, it's not that simple and here is why.

While it is true that Salafi Jihadism is influential and still constitutes an integral part of modern-day violent groups' ideological manifesto, such a hypothesis presumes that all violent groups in Egypt are strictly Salafist —which is not accurate.

According to data collected from Maryland University's Global Terrorism Database, Tahrir Institute's Security Watch Program as well as other unclassified media reports, the period between 2011 to 2020 have witnessed the birth of sixteen groups[2] that have declared the use of violence in Egypt albeit with varying degrees and different agendas. Eleven of them are homegrown with minimal to no publicity known regional or global ties. And while seven of the sixteen adopt one version or another of a jihadist Salafism, the rest of the groups seem to use far less religious tone. In fact, four of them adopt no jihadist Salafist, or even religious discourse in their public communique or media releases at all.

An example of these groups is the Revolutionary Punishment Movement (RPM), which, according to data from their official statements, have carried out over 140 attacks against state targets and state officials exclusively. Despite government efforts to link them to the jihadist groups, the group has eschewed any religious tone in their public statements and communiques. In their four-minute inaugural video release, the masked spokesperson did not mention one single word that could associate the group to any religious affiliation of any kind. Instead, the whole account was focused on the overwhelming injustices that the people of Egypt have been suffering, namely those who were associated with political activists.

A thorough study of Revolutionary Punishment Movement (RPM) media statements and audiovisual content reveals some important indicators that could explain their mindset and help situate them in the political violence spectrum. Among the most important observations is the way they start off their statements. Instead of a classic jihadist opening that often starts with stating the name of God or a Qur'anic verse that highlights the significance of the group's deed, RPM opens their statements with "In the name of the revolution." Such an opening is almost unheard of especially when the rest of the statement addresses issues of injustices and grievances without making one single reference to god, jihad, faith, or Islam.

This is a completely different tone from what we can see in classic jihadist groups like Al-Qaeda and the Islamic State and their affiliates in Egypt who use a heavily religious tone in their speeches and media releases. Wilayat Sinai (WS), which is a branch of the Islamic State in Egypt's Sinai Peninsula, follows the styling guide of its mother organization. Starting with citing the name of God and/or a Qur'anic verse that relates to the particular statement's core matter. The operations carried out by Wilayat Sinai (WS) are regularly framed as a martyr mission in which one person is sacrificing his soul for the sake of defending his religion and glorifying the god. On the contrary, RPM framed their operations as "revolutionary/guerrillas ops" as opposed to "martyr ops"—which is the term used by other jihadist groups. Reporting on their attack in Fayoum on August 29, 2015, RPM dedicated the attack neither to god nor to Islam, but they stated that "this is just a humble gift from RPM to all revolutionary activists in Egypt."

In their statement on January 22, 2015, RPM titled their announcement as "*Feda'youn Qadmoun*" where they announced a new pattern of attack that involved self-bombing. In Egypt, the term "*Feda'youn* (or guerrilla) operations" is historically associated with anti-colonial militants who resisted the

British occupation, and later the Israeli occupation in Egypt. The term has a strong connotation to nationalist patriot groups rather than Islamist violent groups.

In the table below, I highlight examples of how the same "action" is framed in two different ways in the statements of RPM and WS.

Table 2.1. Comparison of wording and terminology between Revolutionary Punishment Movement and Wilayat Sinai

Action Description	Revolutionary Punishment Movement (RPM)	Wilayat Sinai (WS)
Opening a statement/ media release	In the name of the revolution	In the name of god
Attacks	Guerilla ops	Martyr ops
Calendar used to document events	Georgian calendar	Islamic Hijri calendar
Reference to Egyptian Military and Police	Criminals/other derogatory terms	Apostate/Renouncers (Kufar) (Murtadeen)
Language	Egyptian Slang	Arabic Fus-ha
Overall tone	Retribution from state	Retribution from state
Discourse	Nationalist-revolutionary	Religious jihadist
Group objective	Justice, resistance	Jihad, justice, Islamic Sharia

The table above shows the variance in terminology chosen by the different violent groups in Egypt. Details as little as a group's decision to date-stamp their statements in the Georgian calendar, which is commonly used in Egypt among the public as opposed to the Islamic Hijri calendar, which indicate a certain ideological devotion and religious lineage.

Similarly, groups like RPM, the Execution Brigade, and Helwan Brigade chose to speak in slang Egyptian—rather than Fus-ha Arabic which is commonly used by more jihadist groups—shows these groups are actively trying to disassociate themselves from the more religiously affiliate insurgents. Even though some researchers suggest strong ties between Revolutionary Punishment Movement (RPM) and the Muslim Brotherhood, there is no solid evidence that connects the two groups together. Perhaps a more compelling scenario would insinuate a strong presence of Muslim Brotherhood offshoots in the core body of the Revolutionary Punishment Movement, rather than a structural association between the two organizations.

And while groups like Revolutionary Punishment Movement, the Execution Brigade, and Helwan Brigade use a rather nationalist discourse, other groups adopted a Salafi jihadist discourse. But groups who subscribe to Salafi jihadist ideology such as Islamic State's Sinai Province, Al-Morabtoon, and Al Fourqan Brigades, do not share an identical understanding of its provisions.

In fact, many of the Salafi jihadist groups have some fundamental disputes on some very critical issues, such as the legitimacy of targeting civilians.

Al-Qaeda and its affiliates for instance adhere to a form of the Salafi jihadism that permits the use of lethal force against their perceived enemies—including Muslim civilians. Al-Qaeda leadership and its religious scholars often cite the historic work of the classic Islamic thinker, Ibn Taymiyyah whose writing and *fatwas* on the legitimacy of killing civilians—either as direct targets or as collateral—has been at the heart of debates among Muslim scholars for centuries. On the other hand, local groups in Egypt like Ajnad Misr for example, who also subscribe to a Salafi jihadist ideology as well, spare civilian personnel from their fight against the state as long as those civilians are not state officials or partnering with the government or its representatives.

Furthermore, the Salafist jihadi discourse itself that forms the ideological basis for groups like Wilayat Sinai or Al-Qaeda groups has also evolved over the years. From the thirteenth century's Ibn Taymiyyah, to the eighteenth century's Ibn Abdel Wahab, to the twentieth century's Sayyed Qutob all the way to modern-day jihadist discourse. Mazoz (2018) who analyzed the changes that the jihadist discourse went through over the years, demonstrates the characteristics of the classic forms of jihadi discourse. He finds that the classic discourse was focused on fighting the sinful practices within Muslim societies and how to deal with corrupt Muslim scholars. Gradually, the discourse witnessed different leaps, notably during Ibn Abdel Wahhab's time where the jihad expanded and engaged in political alliances and partnerships, but it wasn't until Sayed Qutb in the twentieth century that the jihadist discourse was appropriated to meet the rapid post-colonial changes in many Muslim countries and address issues that were at the periphery of its priorities.

Yet even with Qutb's landmark work, a solid governance system in Islam was absent or at best overlooked (Qutb 1988). It wasn't until the rise of the Islamic State that issues of an Islamic political model and extreme details of governance made it to the center of the jihadists discourse. Such changes in the discourse that started, as Mazoz (2018) argues, with criticism and calls for abolishing existing apostate regimes, but have continued to evolve to respond to, interacted with, and show astonishing flexibility in bending to keep up with the global changes and to serve different purposes.

The changes in the discourse together with great disparities among the jihadist groups shows that Salafi jihadism has different versions and understandings. Thus, putting all modern-day violent groups in one group, and assuming they are all coming from the same ideological background thus behaving in an identical manner, is utterly flawed and will misguide the research efforts.

As demonstrated above, the absence of strong jihadist discourse in groups like RPM is an indication of how little role religion has played in influencing or fueling the institutional commitment of these groups to take up arms. But it is equally important to examine, not just the institutional commitment to the ideology, but also the commitments of the participating individuals to such an ideology. In other words, I needed to observe two factors: 1) How much did the ideological (in this case jihadist) narrative(s) contributed to the decisions of Ramy and his mates to take up arms; and 2) If any, how much of this jihad was politically/socially motivated as opposed to driven by godly orders to fight the apostate?

"What do you think of Ibn Taymiyyah's work?" I asked Ramy.

"I haven't read any of his work to be honest with you," answered Ramy who didn't seem bothered to reference any Salafi jihadi literature. Ramy was rather focused on expressing his own emotional and traumatic experiences rather than preaching for the establishment of some Islamic order.

Unlike Ramy, Hussein was familiar with some literature by Sayed Qutb and Ibn Taymiyyah. Perhaps his background as a member of the Muslim Brotherhood gave him an edge in this field, although Hussein said that the Muslim Brotherhood never formally offered Sayed Qutb books in their teaching sessions when he was a young caliber. It was his own passion to read is what led him to Sayd Qutb's books. But despite his familiarity with Qutb's work, Hussein didn't bring up Qutb's work as much as he talked about Qutb's experience as a prisoner who was tortured and executed in 1966 during Gamal Abdel Nasser's era (1954–1970). It was as if Hussein saw something in common with Qutb's trajectory, as he was once a member of the Muslim Brotherhood and ended up tortured by the state.

Qutb wasn't just an influential Islamist theorist. He was seen as an idol who stood up to the regime of former Egyptian President Gamal Abdel Nasser and didn't backdown against Nasser's intimidation which landed him in jail, and subsequently to his execution in 1966. And while Qutb's writing, especially his manifesto on political Islam "*In the Shades of the Qur'an*," has indeed inspired several generations of violent jihadists, Qutb's journey as a resilient prisoner inspired even those who did not read thoroughly his books or were completely acclimated with his worldviews.

"We are not after establishing a caliphate or even an Islamic order," Ramy explained, "we are not the Islamic State or Al-Qaeda." Out of the sixteen groups that were established in Egypt in the aftermath of the military coup in 2013, only one group—the Islamic State's Sinai Province (WS)—orated about the establishment of an Islamic order to govern and rule. But other groups, who had a glimpse of Salafi Jihadi ideology, like Ajnad Misr, never mentioned any intention to build up an Islamic Caliphate, and never rooted their violence in an exclusive ideological foundation. Instead, Ajnad Misr positioned itself as a revolutionary group fighting against tyrannical rule of the military generals. Similarly, a thorough examination of statements issued by groups like Liwa Al Thawra, Hasm Movement, Helwan Bridges, Popular Resistance Movement, and others, despite some differences, have revealed the same trend of avoiding any allusion to the establishment of an Islamic ruling or orders as to their objective.

Supplementary Enabling Factors

While the Sisi government's main claim was centered primarily around religious fundamentalism, it also mentioned the other vulnerabilities that Egyptian youth have suffered from which made them an easy target for fanatic scholars and violent jihadists to exploit.

Colonel Sameer, a National Security officer interviewed for this study stated that the National Security Agency is keeping an open mind when it comes to dealing with and understanding violent movements in Egypt, though he asserted that the prevailing understanding in Egypt's National Security Agency is all violent groups currently present in Egypt are more or less an offspring from the Muslim Brotherhood and its youth. "Senior Muslim Brotherhood leaders are luring their youth with dreams of establishing the Islamic State," said the Colonel.

Abdel Rahman Ayyash, a researcher focused on radicalization in Egypt says that it might be true that many of today's radicalized youth in Egypt are, or were at some point, affiliated with the Muslim Brotherhood, but there is no material evidence that ties, with certainty, all violent groups in Egypt to the Muslim Brotherhood. The government of Egypt doesn't outsource any independent research centers or academic institutions to provide insights or research of the root causes of violent radicalization in Egypt. In fact, researchers and journalists who work on such topic, in an independent fashion, are often targeted by the state's security agencies. Ismail Al-Eskandrani, a dedicated researcher on violent radicalization in the northern Sinai has been publishing and researching the origins of violent radicalization in Northern Sinai. His analysis conflicted with the government's storyline, which landed him in jail for ten years by a military court (*El-Sayed* 2018).

The government was so adamant about only circulating its side of the story while impeding any other opposing opinions. Amin, a producer who has been working inside one of Egypt's state-controlled media outlets, explained in an interview that any political material that is broadcasted on air must first be cleared by the assigned National Security officer, especially if the topic has anything to do with political violence. "The bottom-line is, as long as you would blame the Muslim Brotherhood, the material would be approved for broadcasting," said Amin who wasn't sure if the National Security truly believed that the Muslim Brothers were really tied to all these violent attacks or it's a state policy to make this claim.

Since the election of President Abdel Fattah El Sisi to office in 2014, the media scene in Egypt—which benefited from limited freedom during Mubarak's rule—has suffered from greater restrictions. In a leaked video speech for Abdel Fattah El Sisi, when he was still the Minister of Defense (2012–2014), while talking to his senior aides he expressed his vision on how the state should take control of all media outlets through creating their own and infiltrating all existing media outlets in order to be able to influence its content. It wasn't long after he was elected president (2014) that he started to do just that. Reporters Without Borders issued a full report in late 2017 detailing the buyout process that the intelligence agencies in Egypt carried out to control local TV channels, media production companies, and printed and online press outlets. Gradually, the state secured ownership of most public and private media outlets, while whatever independent outlets were left were under strict constraints. Such media control, along with silencing of any opposing voices, enabled the government to have the edge in emphasizing its side of the story.

One story—repeated over and over—during a state of emergency, with no opposing opinions, creates a powerful narrative. President Sisi's administration was able to architect strategic control of the media to create a new reality, in this case tying the Muslim Brotherhood exclusively to all political violence in Egypt and describing them as religious fanatics.

Poverty, Economy, and Exploitation

In explaining how the Muslim Brotherhood leadership allegedly recruit and radicalize young people in Egypt, the Egyptian government, through its media outlets, has repeatedly argued that poverty and lack of proper education are what make youth susceptible to violent radicalization. In 2013 and 2014, several media reports broadcasted and published stories that demonstrate how the Muslim Brotherhood exploited the financial distress and the lack of education of some young people to recruit them to commit acts of violence against the state (Akhbar Alyoum 2013).

Poverty, lack of education, and unemployment tops the classical explanations to radicalization, not just in Egypt, but worldwide. Recent study, that examined jihadists in Syria have, however, discredited such correlations and demonstrated the mixed economic and social backgrounds of jihadists (see Mercy Corps Policy Brief 2015). Similarly, Bondokji, Wilkinson, and Aghabi (2016) refers to a study by Rik Coolsaet (2016) on European fighters who moved to Syria explaining that their economic situation—and their well-established careers—was not a factor in their decision to join the armed operations in Syria.

Right before joining the armed insurgency in Egypt, Ramy had a stable career and was preparing to pursue an advanced academic degree. Besides, he comes from a well-off family who owned a business that yielded steady annual profits. Similarly, Hussein who had a promising future career as a physician in a community that respects and appreciates physicians, both socially and financially. So, there is not plausible reason to think that any of these young men needed or were under financial or economic stress that pushed them toward violence. Nor were any of these young men receiving any financial compensation for carrying out these violent attacks—at least per their own testimony and the available data.

But scholars like Turk (2004) look at this line of argumentation differently. He states that political violence is associated with relative affluence and social advantage rather than poverty, lack of education, or other indicators of deprivation. He notes that the prototype of a modern insurgent is usually a young person from a relatively well-off family, who is often motivated by political or ideological resentment rather than economic distress. Suicide bombers increasingly appear to be respected individuals from privileged social classes with stable family and communities. Osama bin Laden, for example, was not just a wealthy educated man whose family business was worth five billion dollars during the early 1980s, he was also a well-respected figure in his community.

In *Why Men Rebel* (1970), Gurr associated political violence to feelings of deprivation that were the result of unfulfilled expectations. He argues that there are three main intersecting factors that explain people's rebellious behavior. First is discontent and outrage; second, readiness to take an action to change the status quo; and third, the balance between the capacity to act or mobilize and the government's ability to repress rebels. Sociologists like Austin Turk (2004) delve deeper into the first factor, exploring people's discontent. This study of discontent often originates from what Alexis de Tocqueville referred to in *The Old Regime and the French Revolution* as feeling relatively deprived when compared with equal peers from other societies or cultures who enjoy a much better quality of life. More specifically the source of discontent is the discrepancy between "value capability," the goods and conditions they think they are capable of getting and keeping on the one hand, and "value expectation," the "goods and conditions of life to which people believe they are rightfully entitled," on the other.

The more educated and affluent their backgrounds, the more impatient they are likely to be with the disappointments of political life where one rarely gets all

that is envisioned and socialized to be knowledgeable about gaps between ideals and realities and to see themselves as significant as participants in political
struggles, higher-class young people especially from liberal families are more
likely than their less advantaged counterparts to become involved in terrorism."
(Turk 2004, 278)

In Turk's view, when people become educated like Ramy, Hussein, and the
like, they develop a well-founded worldview that makes them aware of this
disparity and makes them less tolerant of political strife and human rights
abuses at home, ultimately becoming more frustrated. Alexis de Tocqueville
(1955), for example explains that the revolution began not in the poorest
regions of France, but those where people were doing well, and their lives
were improving.

Many scholars, on the other hand, have criticized this approach that focuses only on socioeconomic factors, and assumes that grievances are enough
reason to incite a collective action. Hafez (2003) in his book *Why Muslims
Rebel*, argues that such an approach underestimates the significance of the
mobilizing material resources and committed activists in order to wage a
fight against the state. Similarly, Sageman (2004), who extensively studied
Al-Qaeda fighters, found that relative deprivation is important but not enough
to radicalize people. He argued that radical insurgents, at least in his study of
Al-Qaeda fighters, seem to have been motivated by rising, not lowering, expectations. He found that well-educated young scholars sought other Muslims
who shared their disappointment with various social conditions, who then
established their own isolated community which led to a socio-intellectual
alienation.

Theorists like Charles Tilly, Theda Skocpol, and Sidney Tarrow long
argued that studying "social and political structures (Skocpol), political mobilization (Tilly), and mass social movements (Tarrow)" should be the focus
when examining mobilization rather than the individual's relative deprivation. Gurr himself acknowledged the shortcoming of his model saying, "in
light of forty years of research and reflection, I think the core of the *Why Men
Rebel* model remains valid but is incomplete."

Empirical findings that studied the relationship between social status (in
the forms of unemployment and annual income) and terrorism (Collins 1975;
Hafez 2003) found no concrete evidence of positive correlation. Krueger and
Maleckova (2003) studied 129 militants of Lebanon's Hezbollah from 1982
to 1994 and found that the fighter members of the group were more educated
and wealthier than Lebanese of comparable age and religion. Krueger and
Maleckova (2003) argued that economic conditions and social status are ir-
relevant in most cases; they bring in the example of the multifaceted conflict
between Israel and Palestine, where they argue that the great majority of

Palestinians were in favor of violence against Israelis, and an equally clear majority of Israeli Jews were similarly in favor of using violence against Palestinians and opposition groups. On both sides, Turk (2004) adds, religious discourse was prevailing and enthusiasm for violence was unrelated to employment status, income level, or educational background.

And while there is not enough valid empirical data on the economic situation of all or most of those who got radicalized in post-2011 in Egypt, the above studies that were carried out on different peer groups along with the firsthand accounts of those interviewed refutes the claim that economic or financial distress is a main driver behind violent radicalization in Egypt.

From all the above, we can presume with greater degrees of confidence that the allegations put forth by the government of Egypt, whether religious fundamentalism, economic distress, or lack of education, did not offer proper explanation to the phenomenon. The stories of Ramy, Hussein, Tarek, Saeed, and others are far more complex than just relying on outdated macro theories that, even if proven right at some point in the history, it doesn't offer answers to the question of post-2011 violent radicalization in Egypt.

Reading through the stories over and over again, one could observe one common factor among all cases which is the fact that all of them experienced an exceedingly harrowing levels of political repression and cruelties. In the forthcoming section, I will examine the effects of state-sponsored political repression and its associated authoritarian practices on both, well-established social movements as well as independent individuals.

When we think of political repression, we usually envision the iron fist of the state with all that entails. And while this image isn't wrong at all, scholars often like to underscore that repression is much more than that (Pape 2005; Turk 2004; Ben-Yehuda 1993). It manifests in forms of discriminatory policies, sustained alienation of certain segments of the society, marginalization, etc. (Iannaccone 1997; Zidan 2009; Juergensmeyer 2003; Stern 2003; Pape 2005).

Turk (2004) and Ben-Yehuda (1993) argue that political violence is the eventual product of an escalating (and unresolved) political conflict, whether a state-to-state war or guerrilla-style warfare. Iannaccone (1997) adds that a political component must be included in order to create a congested environment that ultimately breeds violence. Pape (2005) claims that more than 95 percent of deadly attacks in his study (1990–2005) were motivated by political secular rather than religious fundamentalist goals, aimed at compelling governments to meet certain political demands.

Citing Latin American movements, Robben (2007) finds that the political violence that swept over Argentina for decades, particularly the ferocious state-led crackdown on protests, forced disappearances, torture, and numerous political assassinations, led to trauma, and that trauma bred violent reaction and mobilization of guerrilla wars. Similarly, LaFree and Ackerman 2009 demonstrate a positive correlation between authoritarian regimes who use excessive violent measures to repress their opposition and the rise of violent radical groups. They argue that when autocrats feel threatened by a rising competitor, they often use their state mechanisms (police and military) to repress any potential threats that could undermine their power. Similarly, in *Why Muslims Rebel*, Mohamed Hafez (2003) identifies state-led repression, not just socioeconomic and ideological factors, as the primarily motivation for Islamist militancy.

As he focused on Algeria and Egypt, Hafez argued that decades of state-re-pression and exclusionary policies led Islamist movements to turn to violence as a tool of political participation. Militants used violence to target political and military figures but then expanded in the late 1980s and 1990s to include secular intellectuals, artists, tourists, and noncombatant civilians as targets. And while I agree with Hafez on his analysis of Egypt's radical movements during 1960–1990, we have to be careful when we extend his theory to the contemporary wave of violent radicalization in Egypt (post-2011). Not only because the political climate in Egypt nowadays is influenced by far more complex dynamics than those in the 1960–1990s, but also because not all rad-icalized individuals in Egypt stemmed from exclusively Islamist background.

On the other hand, not all scholars see politically oppressive environments as a source of breeding violence. Goodwin (2006) suggests that state vio-lence is not necessarily a breeding ground for violence because a strong and coercively organized state can disarm its militant opposition by advancing its own bureaucratic repressive capacity, which increases the state's reach into society and enhances its ability to collect and use information. And to a big extent, countries like Egypt, especially under the rule of Abdel Fattah El Sisi has managed to ramp up its capacity to counter groups of political violence.

The problem with such an approach, however, is that it overestimates the state's ability to sustain consistent measures of repression across time and throughout its territories—something that, if not impossible, is at best extremely difficult to achieve. We have seen examples from the USSR and other extremely cohesive state apparatuses collapse, in a matter of few days like the 2011 Arab Spring of Libya (seven days), Egypt (eighteen days), and Tunisia (twenty-seven days).

Besides, using "authoritarian practices" to counter political violence, while on the surface could result in an incremental victory for the state, it doesn't eliminate violent groups or the causes that inspired them in the first place. government capacity, no matter how strong they may appear, has its limitations especially if these groups are located in transnational spaces or border areas, or even in other countries.

Many governments with a gigantic financial, logistical, and military capacity, including democratic regimes, have used varying degrees of violent, inhumane tactics in an effort to eliminate radical violent groups, yet failed to achieve any considerable success. The United States "War on Terror" that started in the aftermath of the 9/11 attacks targeting violent groups like Al-Qaeda, the Taliban, and later the Islamic State and other groups, and have deployed multiple violent and coercive tactics including systemic abuses while in captivity like the "Enhanced Interrogation Technique" which is basically a fancy name for "torture" during interrogation with members of these groups (McCoy 2007).

In 2002, then-U.S. President George W. Bush signed a memorandum stating that "the Third Geneva Convention guaranteeing humane treatment to prisoners of war did not apply to Al-Qaeda or Taliban detainees, and a December 2002 memo signed by former Defense Secretary Donald Rumsfeld, approving the use of 'aggressive techniques' against detainees held at Guantanamo Bay, as key factors that led to the extensive abuses" (Montgomery 2008).

Egypt, one the U.S. closest allies in the Middle East was one of the select black sites used by the U.S. intelligence to perform and carry out enhanced interrogation techniques for U.S.-captured suspects of terrorism (Burke 2004). It's not that Egypt needed any new ideas on how to torture and interrogate its detainees, but the involvement of a leading democratic superpower like the United States in such manner gives political backing to countries who systematically use these techniques and normalize authoritarian practices as a means of "counterterrorism."

And, despite the decades' worth of systematic torture committed by several governments to end "terrorism," we still witness the birth of newer, even stronger, generations of violent groups. This, with absolutely no doubt, means that the violent tactics and authoritarian practices that were used by government are not only impractical, but could also be counterproductive and ultimately becomes grounds to legitimize the armed insurgency against these states. When the United States started its war on terror in 2003, its biggest and most ferocious enemy was Al-Qaeda. Now, many years later, not only is Al-Qaeda still standing, but newer groups like the Islamic State was born and was in control of larger territories in both Syria and Iraq—at one point they controlled more territories than the government of these countries.

This leads us to a central point in this book. Perhaps it's not political repression per se that, on its own, breeds violence, but the practices that results from a repressive political climate. To understand this further, we need to carefully review Egypt's history of political repression. Not just to understand how and why this repression accumulated, but also to identify its characteristics and analyze their possible contribution to the process of violent radicalization.

The Nexus of Repression, Trauma, and Shame

Tyrannical practices are staple at any dictatorship. The consecutive presidents of Egypt, since early 1950s, have maintained a repressive environment to control society and ensure regime stability and longevity. They did so through empowering and investing in the state security apparatus that used wide cruel tactics against their political adversaries. And despite the different style and tactics of each of these presidents, they remained more or less on the same footsteps (see Fahmy 2005). Egypt's security apparatus—namely the military and police have gradually become to the front and center of the political scene. While military guided the bigger picture and general policies, police had their hand on the domestic affairs, not much criminal policing as much as political policing and social control.

Several international organizations have investigated Egypt's security apparatus' practices over the years. These investigations have often accused Egypt's police forces of committing brutality, suppressing opponent voices, directly undermining human dignity, spreading torture, allowing unjustified detention, and putting political activists under unlawful surveillance. Police became the tough arm of the consecutive military presidents to suppress, detain, torture, and even kill those who oppose the military ruler. Under the provisions of the Emergency Law, political activists have been detained and thrown in jail without arrest warrants and for unlimited periods of time. El Nadim Center for the Management and Rehabilitation of Victims of Violence—an independent Egyptian organization—published in its annual report for 2006 and found that:

> Torture in Egypt is practiced in all police stations, security offices, metro stations and university campuses. Police officers sometimes rent furnished apartments as a place to torture their victims "at ease." The practice of torture is not confined to a specific time frame. It has been happening over long periods of time to the extent that Egyptian and International Human Rights organizations have come to describe it as "a systematic state policy." (El Nadim 2006, 33)

The lack of accountability for police officers who commit violations have given them free rein in practicing their abuses. Police brutality has become almost a standard practice over the years. Not just against political activists and public figures whose influence undermine the regime, but also against average individuals who dare to oppose a police officer's commands. In July 2007, a short video clip was publicized that featured a twenty-one-year-old Egyptian minivan driver Emad El Kebir being forcefully sodomized with a rubber stick by a group of police officers and corporals while he was detained in a police station. Not only did the police torture Emad, but they also willingly sent his torture footage to Emad's fellow drivers and family members to warn them that a similar fate could face any of them if they disobey police officers.

Emad's public outcry about the incident was an unusual reaction in a cultural frame where sense of shame usually prevents men and women from portraying themselves as "rape" victims because it connotes weakness, dishonor, and humiliation. Emad's story is not unique, civil society organizations (both locally and internationally) have documented thousands of cases of torture and abuses that took place at the hands of the state.

Decades of political repression and authoritarianism have certainly left a mark on Egypt's modern history. While repressive environments impact societies in their entirety—from freedoms to political structure—it is important to explore what these authoritarian practices do to individuals who experience them directly.

Clinical studies that examined political prisoners in repressive countries, especially those who were exposed to severe levels of torture, have detected that trauma, emotional distress, rage, and grief are among the most observed symptoms in those individuals (Fischman 1991). Torture comes in different shapes and forms. Article 1 of the 1984 United Nations Convention Against Torture:

> Any act by which severe pain or suffering, whether physical or mental, is intentionally inflicted on a person for such purposes as obtaining from him or a third person, information or a confession, punishing him for an act he or a third person has committed or is suspected of having committed, or intimidating or coercing him or a third person, or for any reason based on discrimination of any kind, when such pain or suffering is inflicted by or at the instigation of or with the consent or acquiescence of a public official or other person acting in an official capacity. It does not include pain or suffering arising only from, inherent in or incidental to lawful sanctions.

The main objective of such torture, Somnier and Genefke (1986) (Fischman 1991) argue, is the destruction of the personality of the victim. This comes in line with the testimony that Major Alaa shared earlier in this book "the motive is not often to extract information but rather to inflict pain to humiliate the subject and make them feel helpless and useless."

"I offered to sign any papers or confessions they wanted me to say to avoid torture. But even that, would not dissuade them from torturing me," said Ramy. "It's as if they enjoy the process of humiliating us."

The magnitude of torture is immense and goes beyond the visible symptoms. As Gurr and Rasmussen (Marcussen et al. 2001) described it, torture doesn't only target the victim's body or mind but reaches the victim as a whole, his body, his personality, and his relationship with society. It creates a traumatic scar that will live with the victims for many years (C. Williams and der Merwe 2013) and could alter their behavior, possibly leading to violence toward their friends, families, and others as they lose their faith and trust in their surrounding communities.

The depth and breadth of trauma varies from one individual to another, but the severity of its symptoms could also depend on how the victims address it—or if they acknowledge its existence in the first place. Other than the little informal support they received from their fellow inmates or friends and family members, neither Ramy, Hussein, nor Tarek received any psychological therapy or any other forms of emotional support and rehabilitation either in prison (which is unthinkable) or even after their release.

Nightmares, flashbacks, unexplained body aches, and deep sense of humiliation were experienced by Ramy during his imprisonment and thereafter. This sense of humiliation was also expressed by the other interviewees and in other studies on post-revolutionary Egypt (see Matthies-Boon 2017). McCauley (2017) defines humiliation as a combination of both anger and shame. He makes a clear distinction between humiliation generated from situational distresses (like devaluation, injury, and failure) and the emotional experience of humiliation, in which the synergism of outrage and shame produces a combined effect greater than the sum of their detached effects. Modern appraisal theory (Schulz and Lazarus 2012) characterizes humiliation as a container of "thoughts, feelings, physiological reactions, and action tendencies that is associated with perceiving a situation as having a particular importance for well-being" (McCauley 2017).

Culture and society can determine how we understand and react to certain symbols, figures, rituals, values, concepts, and even words—and more importantly—define acts of humiliation. Many elements like history, religion, and tradition interplay to inform our understanding and to guide our behavior in given situations (Goodwin, Jasper, and Polletta 2004; Scheff 2000; McCauley 2017). For example, in Egypt, sexual assaults bring shame on the victim, not the perpetrator. Through a complex narrative, the victim is framed as "unclean" or somehow tainted by the experience, whereas the perpetrator is often characterized as powerful and aggressive; the result is a debilitating and shaming sexual assault stigma that sticks with the victims to humiliate them and their families throughout their life.

Although the concept of shaming a sexual victim is appropriately deemed perverse and misguided by many, due to the strength of the narrative and social understanding of sexual assault in Egypt, it is incredibly difficult for any victim or small group to alter this cultural concept in any significant way. Thus, victims of sexual assault in Egypt often suffer from this stigma for the duration of their lives, without reprieve.

The nexus between shame, anger, and humiliation is central in understanding human behavior in such situations (McCauley 2017). Victims of this syndrome often perceive themselves as "ridiculed, scorned, insulted, degraded, dishonored and devalued" (Lazare 1987). Empirical studies by Katz (1988) show that "shame, anger, and humiliation" are always at the root of violent behavior. This violent tendency can be even more pressing if the perceived perpetrator is inaccessible (for example, protected by the state, or a powerful family, or fame and not being held accountable for their deeds in a court of justice).

The work of sociologist Thomas Scheff (2000; 2007) is particularly useful in this context. Scheff examined the connection between individuals (psychotherapy sessions) and nations (Hitler's discourse) and discovered a cycle of anger and shame. He describes this loop of (anger-shame) as *rage*; "rage seems to be a composite affect, a sequence of two elemental emotions, shame and anger" (McCauley 2017, 432). Scheff elaborates on the social construction of shame and argues that it is understood as the negative opposite of the positive emotional status of *pride*. We feel *pride* when we do things that are socially approved such as achieving academic success, career accomplishments. On the opposite side is *shame*—often experienced with failures, rejection, or the socially and culturally disapproved acts.

Put simply, both pride and shame are socially and culturally constructed concepts. Basically, this means that what makes an individual proud/ashamed depends on the society or the culture in question. The same act that can make someone proud in a liberal society for example, may well be shameful in another more conservative culture. Cooley's (1922) analysis of the nature of the self-echoes this understanding. He argues that the human consciousness is *social* because we construct it when we look at ourselves through the lens of the society and the perception of others.

Although Goffman in *Interaction Rituals* (1967) does not explicitly mention the term *shame*, he talks about *embarrassment*—usually associated with shame—(as a social institution) that is central to changing human conduct as it generates patterns of emotionally laden interactions that reproduce this institution. Scheff (2000) explains that embarrassment as treated by Goffman (1967) is one of the many forms or manifestations of shame. This is a central theme in Nadim Centre's (1999) study on victims of rape in Egypt, of which 98 percent of the victims mentioned that they felt embarrassed to meet or confront the society after their rape incidents. The report explains that this research demonstrated that victims of sexual assault feel that the society will never look at them as "normal" again, that they assume—rightly or wrongly—they will be treated as people with shameful records, and thus their chance of normal life is slim. Adler's ([1907–1937] in Scheff 2000) psychoanalytical approach suggested that victims of sexual assault are more likely to feel inferior and alienated by their own societies. Nadim Centre (1999) further observed that, in Egypt, this can manifest in an inability of female victims to find a spouse, because the men who ascribe to the culturally constructed concept that shames the victim deem these women as unfit for marriage.

Shame is key in understanding the transformation in our study. Tarek recounts the moments he knew about the police's involvement in sexually assaulting his fiancé by saying "it was as if you set me ablaze, except that I decided to transfer this fire to people who assaulted my fiancé [the police]." Tarek's experience is a poignant example of Goffman's emphasis on embarrassment (or, in this case, shame) as a social institution that emerges and is sustained through social interaction (i.e., external action). It is a social-psychological phenomenon that blurs the distinction between "inside/ outside." As a culturally constructed emotion, it is not necessarily just the perceived culture at a personal, individual level, but rather as an institutionalized phenomenon—it is embedded in (structures of) social relations. The war born inside Tarek when he learned of his fiancé's incident, transformed from internal angst and rage to an external battle ground.

Tarek burst onto the street when he decided to take revenge on behalf of his family and fiancé. When I asked him about this, he explained that "in Upper Egypt (southern culture), revenge is embedded in our culture, and I decided to avenge for her to clean the name and to regain our family pride." Tarek's reaction and thirst for revenge for this humiliation is a familiar pattern that is well explained in Lewis's (1971)[3] work that describes the sequential connection between shame and outrage.

NOTES

1. Name Changed.

2. Revolutionary Punishment Movement, Liwa Al Thawra, Hasm Movement, Helwan Brigades, Forqan Brigades, Molotov, Technical Committees, Al-Morabtoon, Ajnad Misr, Jund Misr, Jund El Islam, Popular Resistance Movement, Army of Islam, Anasr El Islam, Wylat Sinai (formerly Anasr Bait El Makds), and Execution Brigades.

3. In her study of emotion in psychotherapy, 1971, Lewis systematically rated cues for shame and rage, moment by moment, in audiotapes for several hundred sessions. For this purpose, she used the Gottschalk-Gleser scale (1969) for rating emotions in verbal texts.

Chapter Three

The Pursuit of Vengeance

One of the observed common denominators among the interviewed individuals is that they are all emotionally charged. It is not hard to understand why. They each had deeply held feelings of injustice after having experienced extrajudicial killing, arbitrary arrests, torture, loss of family members, assault on family members, and the like.

In a normal circumstance, only one factor of the aforementioned is enough to easily push a person into a state of severe emotional distress and possibly lead to severe trauma. But consider the sequence of actions experienced by these men; in the case of Ramy for example: (1) brother wrongfully arrested, (2) mother humiliated by police officers for daring to question that arrest, (3) his own unlawful arrest without cause, (4) tortured at the hands of the state, (5) thrown into the quagmire of Egypt's worst jails, and (6) learning of his mother's death while still in jail. All of these elements were experienced back-to-back in the complete absence of basic due process or human rights considerations, much less anything that remotely resembled justice.

Keywords and expressions collected from the interviews demonstrate the inner dialogue and emotional turmoil these men experienced. Ramy, for instance, talks about being outraged for the injustices he suffered from, but also talks about the guilt he carries for being a reason in his mother's death. Hussein raises the feeling of betrayal he felt from the institutions [military, police, judiciary] who should have protected him and upheld his rights, but instead, they were the reason behind every perceived injustice he grieved and every trauma he suffered. Tarek's feeling of outrage for his fiancé's incident were intertwined with a cultural paradigm of shame and honor doubled—which further exacerbated his emotional strain.

Emotions and emotional distress have generally been overlooked—or sometimes even discredited—by scholars of political and social studies.

Building on Weberian notions, scholars could not associate emotions with rational acts. Either because emotions are seen as unreliable explanans for complex social phenomenon or because emotions are too meek to invoke collective violent behavior.

Even when there was some recognition of the role of emotions in social studies, it was often confounded with other motives that are seen more rational (Scheff 2000). Scholars often tried to look for a more rational, quantifiable, variable to explain social issues or even worse, strip individuals from the influence of their own emotions and claim that these emotions are mirroring the group/crowd's dynamics and passion (Goodwin, Jasper, and Polletta 2001). Craig Calhoun (2001) thinks that the reason behind this problem is that "emotion" has been seen a property of "psychology" and was not recognized as basis for deciphering social mobilization or the dynamics of collective action.

But this trend has been contested recently. In *Passionate Politics: Emotions and Social Movements* Goodwin, Jasper, and Polletta (2001) revamped the discussion on the role of emotion in social studies. They demonstrate how anger, fear, frustration—even love and compassion—play a critical part in the advent of social protest. Emotions are not just the complex neurological processes that are locked inside our bodies. As Calhoun (2001) argues, emotions are deeply embedded in our biographical experiences and our social interactions.

Emotions, whether outrage, shame, pride, or frustration are essential hinges in the gears of mass mobilization and collective action. They are critical to sustain a group momentum, recruit new calibers, shape their tactics, and even justify their very existence (Goodwin, Jasper, and Polletta 2001; Kemper 2001). Reference to emotions, particularly "anger" has appeared several times in the interviews as an overarching sentiment that encapsulated trauma, pain, and frustration.

Emotions in general are complex. They refer to a wide range of feelings, experiences, and understandings and are greatly influenced by our senses, cultures, languages, frame of references, and aspirations. But anger in particular has an interesting characteristic. It occupies our brain and mental status in order to motivate us to take an assertive action. Anger will not draw until it has been settled (Tarabay and Warburton 2017). This settlement can be through nonviolence such as discussions, talks, negotiations, passive behaviors, legal channels, or very ferocious conduct such physical fighting, inflicting bodily harm upon the adversary, or other forms of vindictive actions. Janne Van Doorn (2018) argues, the operationalizing emotions like anger could lead to a desire to change a perceived "unjust" situation which could transpire through aggression and coercion aimed at the anger-eliciting target (see Van Doorn, Zeelenberg, and Breugelmans 2014).

To understand the nexus between anger and aggression, psychology lends us the General Aggression Model (Allen, Anderson, and Bushman 2018). The model is an integrative framework that incorporates social, cognitive, developmental, and biogeological factors to explain human aggression. It suggests that human behavior is influenced by "knowledge structures" that subsequently shape our decision-making process. Knowledge structures can be a belief system, perceptual schemata, behavioral scrips, or some similar construct. For example, believing that violence—even killing—someone in self-defense is considered "normal" and "ethical."

The authors theorize that there are two main underlying processes in this model. First, proximate processes that explain human episodes of aggression through personal and situational factors that influence human's appraisal and decision making where risk factors (like the presence of a gun or suffering extreme pain) could quickly increase chances of violent aggression, whereas protective factors (like a calmer environment) would decrease the chance of violent escalation. The second is the distal process which works in the background of a proximate process, for instance, biological factors (tendency to engage in violence), cultural norms (that authorize the use of violence in certain situations), victimization, and deprivation.

Applying this model to our case studies highlights higher risk factors like constant pain (both physical through torture and psychological through loss of beloved ones, and feelings of injustice) with almost complete absence of protective factors that could decrease chances of violent escalation. Inhumane conditions inside prison cells, lack of proper sanitation and health care, overcrowded cells, constant humiliation—with no chance to hold officers/prosecutors accountable for any alleged violations—create an even more agitating environment.

The combination of trauma, guilt, anger, and despondency put these individuals in a trigger state—where they were on the verge of embracing radical behaviors. This combination, I argue, comprised the perfect storm that instigated a determination to resolve unsettled grievances. Knowledge structures—particularly sociocultural schemata—would play a key role in guiding the rage of these individuals toward settling this grievance. The paths may have been different, but they all led to one destination: an urge for revenge.

Vengeance

"I trained myself to collect every bit and piece of information about these officers' identity; their pseudonyms, their tone of voice, their ranks, and everything I could put my hands on," Ramy explained.

"I didn't see who they were [because he was blind-folded during interrogation and torture sessions], I didn't know their real names, but I felt their heavy hands on every part of my body," he added as he described that in doing this work, it gave him a reason and a motivation to live another day.

"Motivation?" I asked.

"A motivation to get out of prison so that I can hurt them, the same way they hurt me," he answered.

A desire to retaliate and seek revenge was one common and dominant thread in the stories of Ramy, Hussein, Tarek, and Saeed and others. Revenge is not an end in itself, it's a means to achieve either a denied sense of justice or an absent justice. The concept is described by Bradfield and Aquino (1999) as a disproportionate, emotionally charged reaction to a perceived injustice that is otherwise unsettled. Studies have shown repeatedly that revenge helps achieve a sense of closure or relief from the burden of the trauma in many situations.

Revenge is an ancient concept. In primitive pre-state societies, if person A took person B's hard-earned food of the day, person A would inflict harm on person B to punish him for his wrongdoing, and to dissuade person B from ever doing that again. This is a primitive form of what has evolved into what we now know as the justice system or more generally, the social contract.

The main goal of revenge, Elster (1990) argues, is to establish a sense of justice. In modern states, justice is often served through a judicial process where independent courts of law apply civic laws and rules; the state system is designed to hold individuals accountable for criminal acts (which are essentially acts defined by the society as impermissible offenses). If Egypt's legal system functioned properly and honored both local laws and global human rights treaties, Ramy and the others should have had a system of legal recourse to hold accountable the perpetrators of the crimes they suffered— whether police officers or citizens.

But no such opportunity was afforded to these men, so they were left to consider how to achieve what they perceive as "fair settlement" when the state's justice system failed to render any semblance of legitimate justice. Some scholars argue that individuals in these situations resort to other alternatives such as customary law councils, tribal traditions, and community arbitrations, as well as other forms of culturally approved mechanisms (i.e., revenge). People summon cultural legacies to guide their behavioral responses when justice systems are ineffective or politicized. Some of these responses can authorize people to serve justice through their own hands and according to their own cultural beliefs, which often determine and guide the proceedings of how justice shall be achieved (Girard 2007).

Over time and in different settings, revenge has evolved and taken many different forms. The concept is defined in each setting to accommodate the unique aspects of each culture or community. In Egypt, revenge has been practiced for centuries as a means of achieving communal justice, particularly in areas where government has less control. Aḥmad Abu Zayd's (1965) ethnographic study of Egyptian society notes that *revenge* (tha'r) flourishes particularly in Egypt as an alternative system of justice. It becomes a means of regaining pride and warding off shame. Plotting, seeking, and achieving revenge is also an exercise of solidarity by a social group whose member has suffered harm or wrongdoing by an external aggressor. It also acts as a deterent and prevents future protracted conflicts; something that Scheff (2000) also argued in his *Bloody Revenge*. Specifically, Scheff argues that protracted conflicts often develop from unacknowledged feelings of shame and rage. The initial suppression of the conflict grows with time, which leads to different forms of violence years later.

Tarek, whose fiancé was assaulted during detention, decided to take action on behalf of his family and fiancé. He explained that "In Upper Egypt (southern culture), revenge is embedded in our culture, and I decided to avenge for her to clean the name and to regain our family honor." "It is not an option, it's a duty," he added.

Sarah, an activist who worked closely on documenting cases of female prisoners being assaulted by police officers in detention facilities stated in an interview that female prisoners whose families from Upper Egypt often avoided raising any legal complaints against officers who assaulted their detained relatives. "No one has faith in any accountability in any," she said, but also these families would carry out revenge against these officers themselves. "I used to receive phone calls from family members of imprisoned women, stating that they have now served justice," said Sarah. Which often means they have murdered the person they suspect had assaulted their relative.

Stories of Ramy and others highlights a strong desire to revenge and retaliate from those who inflicted pain, shame, and humiliated them or their loved ones and went unpunished. But this underlying desire is not just visible in the interviews and testimonies of the interviewees, but also the statements and press releases of several violent groups in Egypt. A closer look at statements and media releasees from five violent groups across the political violence spectrum reveals even more powerful data, suggesting that an obvious desire for revenge was the primary motivator for action as opposed to the classic narratives of jihad—that traditionally revolved around divine orders and ideologically driven motivations.

In the table below are findings from a random sample of ten media releases of five violent different groups, wherein all keywords, terms, expressions, and cultural concepts that directly or indirectly referred to either concepts of jihad or revenge were taken into account.

Table 3.1.   Comparison of narratives among five different violent groups in Egypt

Group Name	Narratives of Revenge	Narratives of Jihad
Revolutionary Punishment Movement	45	1
Hasm Movement	31	12
Liwa Al Thawra	25	10
Ajnad Misr	14	7
Sinai Province	7	9

The data analysis showed an evident dominance of revenge narratives over jihad. Keywords like "revenge," "regaining missed pride/honor," "retribution," "vengeance," and "justice" frequently appeared in the press releases and videos. Other jihad narratives found less frequently were "jihad," "god's orders," and "supporting/defending Islam."

Even groups that adopt a more religious tone in their discourse have based their ideological justification on issues of revenge and retaliation. For example, Ajnad Misr's public discourse (both written and audiovisual), emphasized a revenge narrative, rather than a jihadi discourse. The "Retribution Is Life" video repeatedly showed several scenes of police officers assaulting nonviolent demonstrators in multiple instances—each of those scenes was followed by a fierce response from Ajnad Misr members to avenge for the "innocent citizens" assaulted by the police. The video was then dedicated to the mothers who lost their sons and daughters in police violence.

Ajnad Misr's inaugural statement stated that the purpose of their establishment was to "avenge from the aggressors who crippled the progress of the [2011] revolution."[1] Another statement stated that "we are targeting senior security officers who were involved in the violent dispersal of Rab'a sit in, in order to retaliate for our proud women who were captured by the state."[2]

These groups seem to have been comprised of individuals with varying degrees of grievances, but with a similar desire to revenge from the same general perpetrator (e.g., the state or police/military officers) and have joined together to settle their revenge pleas. Ibrahim Halawa, age twenty-one, was arrested after security forces broke up the 2013 sit-in protest in Rab'aa, Cairo, and was recently acquitted after four years of imprisonment in Egypt; he recently shared his experience with the *Wall Street Journal*. In his interview, Halawa confirmed that dozens of cellmates adopted violent thoughts during their brutal captivity in the jails. "Many of them [prisoners] were engineers, students and doctors who just wanted to get home to their families—but after all those years of being in jail with no explanation, many just wanted revenge" (Lagon and Puddington 2015).

Revenge bestows itself as a powerful opportunity—that is culturally and ethically justifiable—for enraged individuals to seek retribution after being exposed to extreme levels of humiliation and abuse during their imprisonment. The role of institutions is key in shaping the social context in which emotions are culturally constructed (Goodwin, Jasper, and Polletta 2001). Security officers seem to also be aware of this process. In the interview with officer Sameer, he mentioned that interrogation officers usually start with physical torture because such practices break the suspect's will early on through humiliating and degrading them—and that makes the officers job easier.

"It's not that officers love to torture people," said the officer. He explained that the overwhelming number of suspects that officers have to interrogate on daily basis and the pressure the officers fall under [from the political leadership] to foil future attacks and eliminate the dangers of these suspects as quickly as possible, makes "torture" a catalyst in extracting information to help guide the investigation. The officer also argued that beating up, torturing, and humiliating suspects in these kinds of cases is "normal" and acceptable.

"These people go out in the street to kill us and kill innocent civilians, so I think it's fine to torture them," added the officer.

Effects of torture methods and tactics vary over time. What triggered a prisoner's sense of indignation or humiliation at the beginning of his imprisonment is different than what triggers it after a few weeks. "In the beginning, beating parties were the worst, later—beating became an act of mercy because officers could do worse than this by electrocuting us, stripping us naked and lashing us, or taking some similarly abusive course of action," Ramy explained.

When physical torture starts to lose its effects with time (and that varies from person to person), officers start deploying psychological torture tactics aiming at even more severe effects. Ramy explains that officers repeatedly threatened prisoners with the safety and well-being of their family members, especially female family members (mother, sister, wife, and daughter) who, in such a conservative culture like Egypt, are socially perceived as precious and should never be subject to such a threat. Even in revenge practices in Upper Egypt, women are always exempted from being a target of revenge. So, involving female family members in such threats is perceived as shaming, humiliating, and dishonorable.

Detention facilities, such as institutions, thus become an important piece in this transformation conundrum. It is where the institutional practices (e.g., various means of torturing and rewarding) and institutional strategies (e.g., those deliberately focused on humiliating, breaking the will of, and controlling its activist captives) culturally construct and, combined with other cultural institutional practices (e.g., religious teaching, military subcultural practices of conscription, and social organizational recruitment), generate the emotions of shame and humiliation (among others)—and subsequently the desire for revenge, that are central to understanding the radical transformation of the nonviolent individuals.

Moral Exoneration

Despite a strong thirst for vengeance, choosing to commit violence is not easy (Collins 2008) or simple; there is a moral and ethical challenge that individuals who are about to become violent must address. A person may commit murder during a flare of rage but may be unable to later justify the act to himself or others. In a study on a group of imprisoned serial murderers, researchers found that "when people feel guilty about a specific behavior, they experience tension, remorse, and regret. This sense of tension and regret typically motivates reparative action—confessing, apologizing, or somehow repairing the damage done" (Tangney 2014).

Gilligan (2003) argues that a sense of guilt and regret, resulting from a particular violent act, will end the violent cycle because people do not continue to commit acts of violence if they feel remorseful for having done so in the past. Thus, inciting violence is not enough to keep it going, rather, seeking moral approval in order to overcome this sense of guilt is necessary to sustain continued acts of violence. For example, in democracies, law enforcement officers commit violence, they sometimes even kill suspects when necessary without—technically—feeling guilt. The reason behind this is their belief that their violence is justified because their actions are for the benefit and security of the society; thus, not only morally and ethically approved, but also encouraged and hailed by their community members and is rewarded by state bureaucracy. Killing one person or two people is considered legitimate as long as it will save the innocent lives of others.

Clandestine violent activities require a great amount of moral and ethical justification (Hafez 2003). When it comes to political violence in particular, Apter (1997) argues that participants need discourse that enables what psychologists like Bandura (1999) call "moral disengagement"—that ultimately facilitates and justifies violent repertoires of contention (Hafez 2003).

> Moral agency is embedded in a broader socio-cognitive self-theory encompassing self-organizing, proactive, self-reflective and self-regulatory mechanisms rooted in personal standards linked to self-sanctions. The self-regulatory mechanisms governing moral conduct do not come into play unless they are activated and there are many psychosocial maneuvers by which moral self-sanctions are selectively disengaged from inhumane conduct. The moral disengagement may center on the cognitive restructuring of inhumane conduct into a benign or worthy one by moral justification, sanitizing language and advantageous comparison; disavowal of a sense of personal agency by diffusion or displacement of responsibility; disregarding or minimizing the injurious effects of one's actions; and attribution of blame to, and dehumanization of, those who are victimized. (Bandura 1999, 193–209)

The common sense of morality is indeed relative. It varies depending on culture, social class, education, and magnitude of the situation. It is a psychosocial process that dehumanizes the perceived enemy (Waller 2006). It contributes to the moral disengagement by which an individual develops a moral justification to use violence. Committing violence then becomes a moral responsibility instead of an immoral offense.

Hisham Ashmawy, one of the most notorious violent militants in Egypt (ultimately becoming the leader of the Al Morabtoon Group) made a statement to explain that he had split from ISIL's Egypt branch (Wilayat Sinai) when they "deviated from the right path."[3] In this instance, Hisham Ashmawy, decided to leave the group he had been a member of, not because they committed violent acts (in fact, he had been an active participant in such violence in the past), but because the group decided on a new affiliation that permitted attacks on civilians. For Ashmawy, violence against civilians—who are not part of the state apparatus—was not justifiable and was a fundamental break with the "right path."

Rationalizing violence is a regular practice and key to other groups, including the most brutal of them, ISIL, whose media releases show meticulous efforts to morally justify their acts of violence—rooting their justification in historical and religious contexts, and citing heroic Islamic ancestors and religious texts to justify and approve their deeds. These examples demonstrate the importance of justifying violence, not only for emerging fighters, but even for ISIL's leading militants who also must be assured, repeatedly, of how their acts are morally justified.

Mohamed Hafez (2003, 156) argues that there are different mechanisms of moral disengagement, such as "ethical justification of violence, advantageous comparison among episodes of violence, and displacement of responsibility for violence." He then sheds light on the ideological framing, using Snow and Benford (1988) who drew on Goffman's (1974) frame analysis, as one important tool to achieve moral disengagement.

A frame is an "interpretative schemata that simplifies and condenses the world out there by selectively punctuating and encoding objects, situations, events, experiences, and sequences of actions within one's present or past environment" (Snow and Benford 1992, 137, cited in Hafez 2003). In our case we can see, across several violent groups, the invocation of emotional framing and moral shock where the group used startling facts and stories to inform the broader society about their opponents, such as recalling torture victims, violent dispersal of protests, extra judicial killings, and the like. Such strategy (Goodwin, Jasper, and Polletta 2001) suggests it is crucial to build solidarity and mobilize support, raise resources, gain loyalty, and create a sense of community and a strong network of allies.

A closer look at Ajnad Misr further illuminates such strategy. Ajnad Misr's media releases always referred to the security apparatus (military, intelligence, and police) as *criminal agencies*. Such framing, throughout their press statements and audiovisual materials, aimed at depicting a plain image of the security officers that they are "criminals and thugs" who must be punished and sanctioned—just like any other criminal. Similarly, in August 2020, actual footage of the assassination of Egypt's former Prosecutor General, Hisham Barakat appeared on a twitter account under the name "The eye of Egypt." The video focused on the state violent dispersal of Rab'a sit-in in 2013 displaying multiple images of dead protesters and their bodies in the street. As an audio background, the video maker used the voiceover from the government statement when spokesperson stated, "The Prosecutor General ordered the dispersal of the square," immediately after that, the footage shows the PG's vehicle being targeted and blown up, as a punishment for his order that led to the death of thousands of protesters in that sit-in.

Hunt, Benford, and Snow (1994) cited in Hafez (2003) argues that this sort of framing does not aim at reproducing shared meanings and grievances, but rather aims at embellishing them in ways that generate collective action. This can be observed in Ajnad Misr's first statement "Al-Qasas Hayat" where they suggested a collective action—for the shared grievance—by quoting the Qur'an: [retaliation is life] has been mainly a mix between religious text and cultural practices. Although the language of the statement is religious, it is primarily centered around issues of revenge and retribution rather than holy wars. Moreover, the selected verses demonstrate reasons and justification that legitimizes retributive justice like, *"And there is for you in retribution [saving of] life, O you [people] of understanding, that you may become righteous"* (Al Baqarah: 197) (translated from Arabic).

A twenty-three-minute video wove together Quranic verses that support the culture of revenge and retribution while recalling all acts of violence committed by police and military officers against peaceful protesters, women, and children since 2013. The communique tried to link an image between state-sponsored violence and divine commands to people, resistance, and retaliation.

In his address to the families of the victims [of the state violence], Hammam Attia, the group leader, stated that "All I am asking you is to avenge, according to the God's provisions, from those who assaulted you and were never held accountable." Attia's construction of a statement that mixed religious and cultural notions exemplifies how cultural codes, not solely religious codes, were used to address their audience. In this instance, rage can be understood as (Goodwin, Jasper, and Polletta 2001, 12) "culturally and socially constructed" rather than a psychological "personality structure." When

Attia, in his video statement, referred to grave violations (including torture, murder, and rape committed by the military regime) he aimed at exploiting a moment of outrage and provided them with solutions that—he argued—are justifiable on both religious and cultural grounds.

Knowledge structures like cultural norms, religious texts, and social traditions are extremely important in offering morally accepted solutions like revenge. Not only that, but also providing a customary playbook on the rules and ethics of revenge. For example, in Upper Egypt, revenge circles can take years to end. Joseph Nazir, a native of Upper Egypt's town of Kosheh said in an interview that "If somebody kills a man, the family of the man who was killed has to kill two men from the first family. Then the first family has to kill four men from the second family. And it goes on like this. Sometimes for decades" (Lohr 2016).

Traditions of revenge are also very strict. Women and children are excluded from being targets of revenge. There is no statute of limitations on taking revenge. In more traditional settings, funerals are not held for the victim, until someone has successfully taken his revenge. But more importantly, targets of revenge are not randomly or arbitrarily selected. They must be either the perpetrator or a first degree relative to the person who committed the act, not just random related family member.

Carefully and clearly identifying targets is a trait of most post-2013 violent insurgency. One of the most important differences between post-2013 violent groups and older (late twentieth century) violent groups was that the older groups were either directly targeting civilian noncombatants or, at the very least, having higher tolerance for collateral civilian casualities. Older groups like Al Takfir w El Hijra, Islamic Jihad Group, The Islamic Group, and others have, over many years, targeted Muslims and non-Muslim civilians for ideological, religious, and political reasons. Such a pattern of attacks put these groups in direct confrontation with the society—not the just the state—which negated any sympathy from average citizens toward these groups which were seen by the community as monsters. Not just the organized large attacks against civilians took place in several locations, but also random attacks against video rental shops, coffeeshops, and others were recorded.

This is not really the case with the newer groups. Statements from Hasm, Liwa Al Thawra, Ajnad Misr, Revolutionary Punishment Movement, Popular Resistance Movement and others all specify in detail who their targets are which are often state actors, particularly police and military personnel or other state officials. Just like the incident mentioned at the beginning of this book where insurgents targeted exclusively military personnel and facilities in such a remote checkpoint.

One debatable point here is how legitimate it is to attack military conscripts (who are drafted against their own will) if they [the conscripts] did not have a choice in the first place to join the military.

Two separately interviewed police officers—who work on issues of counterterrorism in Egypt—have shared an observation in the insurgents' pattern of attacks. In some confrontations, insurgents shoot at conscripts in undeadly spots like their knees, legs, or feet. That way the conscript was taken out of the fight without killing them. In some situations, one officer said, conscripts were given a warning to surrender their weapons and turn in their commanding officers, in return of their safety.

And while there is no data to support the officers' observations, we still can see varying levels of target tailoring, particularly when it comes to who constitutes a civilian and who constitutes a state affiliate target. This is not to claim that those insurgents did not ever attack civilian noncombatants, but rather to show that modern insurgent groups differ in their strategy in targeting civilians, more often than not making an effort to explain why those civilian individuals were chosen. Sometimes they label them as stalwarts or informants to state agencies who have somehow participated in the crimes perpetrated by the state, or that those civilians were collateral causalities who happened to be in the vicinity of the attack.

An example of that was Hasm's attempt to assassinate the former Mufti of Egypt, Aly Gomaa, who was known for his allegiance for the military. But Aly Gomaa is not just any other persona with allegiance to the state. His position as a former Mufti of the state gives him even more prominence in influencing public opinion in justifying the police and military's use of force.

Another prime example was the assassination of Hisham Barakat, who was Egypt's Prosecutor General at the time of his death. Barakat was seen by many political activists as one of the architects in the crackdown on anti-military coup protesters.

"The assassinated Prosecutor General, Hisham Barakat, was one of a significant few who engineered the repressive crackdown on dissenters in the post-President Mohamed Morsi era. Thousands of government critics, peaceful demonstrators, rights' activists and others were detained under his term and sent to courts with multiple—clearly phony—charges that vary from vandalism all the way to threatening national security. Barakat's cruel role in fabricating charges has not only helped President Abdel Fattah El-Sisi get rid of his opposition figures, but more importantly fostered an unprecedented politicization of prosecutions in Egypt. Whether he deliberately intended to do so or not, he remains liable for the implications of such grave results" (Hendawy 2015).

In a long audiovisual statement (2014), Hamam Attia, the leader of Ajnad Misr stated that "We refuse to build big IEDs that could hurt innocent pedestrians. We make our IEDs carefully in ways that when it blasts, it only hits targets without harming innocent civilians." The group also issued a statement,[4] denying their responsibility of any violent attacks that targeted "public services/facilities."

It is important to note the deliberate efforts of these groups to avoid being associated with randomized killing or deviating away from their state targets. It is obvious that they were trying to avoid confrontation with the general population.

Lastly, it is important to note that as much as this "culture of revenge" offers solutions and guidance and validates the violent acts, once you subscribe to the thought, you fall under the pressure of completing it. Nazir states, "If you kill my brother and I don't kill one of your family, I will be ashamed in the village. Everyone will be talking about me and say he's not a man. He couldn't do it. He's not a man. It's for the honor of the family." "The tornado of emotions and social pressures seems to have not ceased at any moment. Nor will the feeling of rage itself ever cease until revenge is achieved or recognized" (Fitzgibbons 1986).

Rational or Irrational?

Extreme torture, murder of family members, unlawful detention, inhumane prison conditions, extrajudicial killing and, more importantly, a complete absence of an independent judiciary system that could remedy these injustices, were all factors that have set the scene for an inevitable tragedy.

While developing my theory that revenge is a primary motivating factor for the turn to violent insurgency from nonviolent protest, it still begs the question: are emotions enough to drive an otherwise seemingly rational, well-educated person from nonviolence to violence? In other words, if this wave of violent radicalization is indeed motivated, at least in part, by an emotional upheaval, does that make this wave categorically irrational in its core?

There is no short answer to that. Resorting to violence, as argued previously, is not an easy decision especially that those radicalized individuals' decision to fight the state was not an abrupt or hasty decision. These individuals spend a long time thinking, rationalizing, planning, and finally deciding to take up arms. Such a decision, I argue, is not an isolated event and should not be analyzed out of the circumstantial cognitive and emotional process in which it occurred. Taking up arms, was merely the ultimate result of several intertwining factors including, but not limited to, emotions, grievances, social-cultural pressure, etc., which, when they dovetailed together, constituted what Wiktorowicz (2004) has described as "cognitive opening" where an individual is prone to radical change of ideas and beliefs previously held.

People like Ramy and many others who once hoped for a bright future and worked hard for it, who then lost everything in a series of tragedies and appalling acts, become more susceptible to taking drastic actions in retaliation for their suffering. This cognitive process behind violent radicalization is not an act of "momentary rage." This is not a fight in a bar or fierce road rage where temper can spark an immediate uncalculated engagement. These individuals were assiduously looking to settle their grievances that has been lingering for months and, in some cases, years.

In the absence of law, they resorted to the customary structures they were familiar with and could offer them a solution, moral justification, and modus operandi to follow. We can see a careful crafting of messaging, identification of targets, plotting, strategizing and planning, and many successful executions for their ops. They feel rewarded when they carry out an operation that achieves its objective, they relieve their agonies, and feel instant gratification after every achievement they make. For them, it is rewarding as it presents a path to perceived victory.

Whether the community this was as rational or irrational would always be a matter of debate. After all, rationality, reasonability, and prudence are subjective perspectives and our assessment to it vary from one person to another depending on several environmental and sociopolitical factors that influence our judgment and reactions. To sum this section up, whether we see violent resistance as rational or not will always be a matter of debate. But to argue that to be a rational human being you have to be devoid of emotion, no one would qualify. Our brains, body, and mind do not function independently from one another. They are all connected and serve each other's purposes.

The Other End

While this book is exclusively focused on the transformation that happens to activists, it is important to shed light at the receiving end of this conflict. Military, police, and other state entities continue to be targets of the attacks. There is no doubt that Egypt's military and police have been involved in some of the worst atrocities against members of several social movements in Egypt but it is also important to note that these entities, despite their systemic abusive policies, are not identical and the groups themselves are not homogenous. Just like activists and pro-democracy supporters, the police and military institutions are ultimately made up of individuals with their own unique experiences, their own perceptions, and their own worldviews. I have, just like many others have, met police and military officers who fundamentally disagree with the practices of their institutions, even if they still hate the Muslim Brotherhood or the January 2011 movement, they do not see a justification to this excessive violence.

Not only that, but many of those who are currently active members of the military and police in Egypt are enlisted and had no choice in the first place to be part of these institutions. Every male in Egypt is required by law to present themselves to the military for mandatory service. With few exception, young men are usually drafted between one and three years to serve in one of the military branches, armies, and bases. *Wasta*—slang for nepotism—plays a key role in where an individual would be stationed, how much backing he gets, how many days off he is allowed, and how long would they serve. *Wasta* is central to many interactions inside the military. Those with weak or no *wasta*, could end up in secluded locations or harsher conditions—like those in the Farafra checkpoint.

If you lack a *wasta*, like many conscripts, it could mean that your boot camp time is going to be difficult, with wretched conditions, and you will be placed in a remote military branch or location. Former conscripts interviewed emphasized that their training in boot camps were focused on "discipline rather than developing skills." The forty-five-day boot camp training provided tailored preparations for civilians drafted into the different military branches. While some training on shooting, survival, and navigation were provided, there was far greater emphasis on commands, marches, uniforms, and military etiquette. "Boot camps provide more education on military life and command chains rather than professional training," said Sameh who had been trained, in theory, on how to use a weapon, but, in reality, only shot six training shots throughout his one-year draft time.

And while military officers receive longer, and more rigorous training, the military's core body consisted of a majority of poorly trained conscripts. Just like the Farafra base where the attack described at the opening of this book took place, only three career military officers of junior rank were present while the nineteen other soldiers were mandatory conscripts.

Conscripts who end up in locations like in Farafra Oasis in the middle of the desert are more likely to lack any *wasta* or senior connections in the military that could have placed them to a better, more comfortable location. Sameh said the difficult conditions that conscripts live in, especially those who have no *wasta*, make them very close to each other—"after all we live in the same misery, in an isolated location, together."

Ayman, another conscript who was drafted during 2013–2014 and placed at a base near the Libyan border, said that conscripts live a very difficult life through no choice of their own [in reference to the mandatory service]. "I don't mind harsh military conditions, but at least we deserve proper training, suitable protective gear, and appropriate food supply."

Numerous studies and personal testimonies have addressed the violations that conscripts experience during their mandatory service time (Gotowicki 1997). Conscripts are often put as front liners of violent confrontations and largely treated as collateral. The studies showed poor treatment of conscripts, the inferior living standards provided to them, the weak training and armament, and above all, the humiliation they experience as part of the military doctrine for new conscripts.

Nader, another conscript between (2011–2012) expressed his "revulsion" toward military service. His mandatory service was in one the military's corporate facilities.[5] He stated that he had never felt more humiliated in his life than during his service: "I never worked for the country, I worked for the officer in charge who made tons of money for his own pocket." As a highly educated man, Nader felt that his energy and skills were wasted in servicing the military officer's personal interests like driving the car for his family members, taking the officers kids to school and back, and even sometimes being forced to clean the summer house of the officer in command. Nader never attempted to rebel or contest the commands because he had witnessed how conscripts can be easily thrown into military jail on charges of "disobeying military orders."

It all boils down to your *wasta*. The higher ranks your *wasta* hold, the easier and more comfortable your mandatory service is going to be. This, among other conditions, is what makes the draft system in Egypt unfair in the eyes of many conscripts. "I feel for those who fell in the Farafra attack, I could have easily been one of them," said Sameh. Poor training, difficult time, and exhaustion of the long days of fasting composed a perfect storm that made them an easy prey for the attackers.

Thus, we end up in a clash between outraged radicalized individuals, killing and murdering other people just because they wear the uniform that represents injustice to them—even though some of those people in uniform didn't have a choice to wear it or be where they are. But the cycle of violence is so venomous that once it's started, it becomes bloodier and less discriminate with time. The friends of yesterday could well be the foes of today if they—somehow—wore the uniform.

Radicalization for All

One key aspect in this book was laying out the severe emotional distress and exceptional circumstances that largely contributed to the violent radicalization of many youth in post-2011 Egypt. Yet one important question remains unanswered: what happened to those who experienced similar exceptional and severe circumstance but did not participate in violent insurgency?

Research on motives of political participation (violent or nonviolent) or the lack thereof have long been discussed among scholars of various disciplines. In sociology, there is particular interest from social movement theorists in understanding, not only the rise and demise of movements, but also what could motivate individuals to join social movements or groupings and what could make them refrain from any political activity altogether?

Indeed, there are many possible explanations to this particular subject, but because collective violent action in its core is a form of social movement—in which a group of people decides to take up arms against their adversaries—it makes more sense to rely on the social movements paradigm to try to explain why some individuals decided to join violent movements while others didn't, despite experiencing similar conditions.

Social movement theories have maintained that social protest—collectively or individually—emerges when there is a sense of injustices or grievance (Tarrow 1994; Orum and Dale 2008; Polletta 2006; Walton 1992). However, the mere presence of injustice and grievances alone are not enough to give rise to a collective action or sustain it. For a movement to successfully be able to mobilize, recruit new calibers, and maintain its momentum, key factors must be present like adequate funding, resources, a personnel, timing, common objectives, and meanings (Orum and Dale 2008). In addition to that, Neal Caren (2007) adds, in his explanation of the political process theory, that some of most important components are the political opportunity, mobilizing structures, framing processes, protest cycles, and contentious repertoires.

Charles Tilly (1978)'s *From Mobilization to Revolution* concludes that chances of participation in a social protest or movement depends on the congruence of three key components: interests, opportunities, and organization. Interest refers to the prospective benefits and rewards that a participant would gain from partaking in a certain movement, while opportunities refer to the status of the adversary's strengths and vulnerabilities in which a movement is likely to capitalize on. Finally, is the organization's unified identity and ability to carry out its objectives. When three components are aligned, chances for individuals to enroll are higher (cited in Caren 2007).

Building on Tilly's foundational work, McAdam (1982) adds the factor of cognitive liberation in which potential participants are liberated from the constraints of the past and feel that the adversary's political system is no longer legitimate and that his or her participation in the movement would have an impact on their enemy.

Another factor is what McAdam refers to as "indigenous organization" which he argues is a potent factor that facilitated both recruitment and mobilization. These are existing organizations—that were established in a prior circumstance—that are still in possession of strong network, resources, and structures that could be bulk recruited. This can be evident for example in the participants of Helwan Brigades, Hasm Movement, Liwa Al Thawra, and the MB's Technical Committees, for example, who were originally members of the Muslim Brotherhood before they organized these spin-off groups. Staniland (2014) argues that preexisting networks help in the formulation of new insurgent groups; nonviolent prewar social movements, political parties, students' unions, etcetera, are all networks that can be effectively repurposed for war against state actors. Similarly, Sageman (2004) argues that social bonds predate ideological convictions. Members of these networks already share knowledge, information, aspirations, and more importantly, goals which make their reassembly easier and faster.

NOTES

1. Ajnad Misr Statement Number 1, January 2014.
2. Ajnad Misr Statement Number 5, April 2014.
3. Hisham Ashmawy statement on YouTube. https://www.youtube.com/watch?v=AbnHvU which has been deleted by YouTube.
4. Ajnad Misr number 15, April 2014.
5. One of the companies owned by the Egyptian military.

Conclusion

Throughout this book, I sought to offer both a cogent answer and a plausible explanation as to how and why select Egyptian activists have converted from nonviolent to violent means of protest in the face of the state. My inquiry explored what conditions and variables set these men on a different course from those who continued to practice nonviolence. Through multiple interviews with various stakeholders, ethnography, and content analysis, I demonstrated some key factors that prompted the fruition of violent insurgency in post-2011's Egypt.

One of the most important leads in this study was to find out how the interviewed individuals viewed themselves in relation to Egypt's 2011 revolution. In other words, do these insurgents see themselves as an extension of the January 2011 revolution, but with different tactical protesting technique? Or, do they see themselves as leading a different movement altogether?

The breadth and width of the 2011 mass protest makes it impossible to think of it as a separate or unrelated movement from the rise of violent insurgency that took place afterward. But despite this causal relationship, there is a shift in the strategic objectives of the two movements. While the 2011 uprising obviously focused on "bread, freedom, and social justice" using mostly nonviolent means of protests, the insurgents in 2013 shifted the objective to a revenge-based vigilante justice movement.

Could we explain that the nonviolent 2011 revolution in Egypt was a separate revolutionary movement from that of the violent movement in 2013? Perhaps, if we think of the leaders of these separate movements as dictating the tactics used by the activists. However, this simple explanation glosses over more nuanced issues. Taking a closer look at the groups, and the individuals within them, highlights the transformative experience each activist underwent in a short period of time. These individuals had held a deeply rooted belief in nonviolence through the 2011 revolution that they then had to overcome in order to adopt the violent tactics following the 2013 military coup. More than simply pledging allegiance to the movement of the time, these people redefined their fundamental value systems and beliefs in order to take up arms. Such an extraordinary transformation in such a short period of time suggests a complex intersection of forces was at play, not simply a change in leadership.

The firsthand accounts told in this book reveal several facets about violent radicalization in modern-day Egypt, particularly in the aftermath of the military takeover in 2013. The relatively rapid transformation that happened to many young people in Egypt was a result of egregious violations at the hand of the state. Ramy, Hussein, and Tarek were all supporters of democracy, active political participants, and seeking a better future for their country.

After a brief state of euphoria in 2011, followed by a crushing defeat in 2013, that then turned into the cause for systemic torture, humiliation, and degradation of their basic to humanity—these once nonviolent activists no longer held hope for a greater future. Having been stripped of their humanity, they become solely focused on vengeance, on achieving some form of justice against the perpetrators of the transgressions they suffered.

Radicalization into violent insurgency doesn't happen in a vacuum and is not an isolated event. It is rather a process that develops through associations embedded within other forms of agency and social interactions. Contemporary literature argues that violent insurgency is not an end on its own, it is merely a proxy that allows other social processes to surf anonymously in a concealment of a person who uses violence for tactical or strategic purposes. To understand this buffer proxy zone, we must explore on the micro-level, the smaller social processes that contribute to the accumulation of radical violent behavior. Randall Collins (2008) argues that violence can best be understood by analyzing the micro-situational dynamics of a situation, not background factors alone. In other words, only by acknowledging the heterogeneity of processes and the various pathways that build up toward collective violence can we understand the unequal effect of these micro-level grievances.

Understanding the conditions under, and means by which, this contributes to a process of violent radicalization characterized by the subsequent use of violent tactics of collective action will explain how groups and movements choose to use violent tactics to exploit political opportunities to recruit potential "calibers" (willing followers) by deploying various dynamic methods and discursive frames.

I suggest that there should *not* be one fixed procedural paradigm or grand theory to explain all radicalization around the world or throughout history as if they are different faces of the same coin. They are not. I cannot emphasize enough how necessary it is to thoroughly explore the details, trajectory, forces, motivations, socialization, and all related factors that contributed to the radicalization of groups and individuals within their own peculiar contexts and political environments. Impulsive suppositions, sweeping generalizations, and oversimplifications of such intricate phenomena would misguide the research efforts and lead to false results and flawed understanding.

"Premature generalizations can be avoided by remembering that each victim of torture comes to therapy with a particular internalized combination of externally determined and intrapsychic conflicts. It is helpful to focus on individuality, even in this context of commonality, and pay attention to individual pre-trauma history, defenses, and style of coping with psychological trauma" (Fischman 1991).

As I present these findings below, I also discuss their implications for the literature on social movements and violent insurgency. I also suggest potentially fruitful avenues for future research.

1. The political process paradigm for understanding social movements suggests that shared grievances are constant in every society and thus, they alone, are not enough to explain the emergence of social movements— whether violent or nonviolent. An important finding of this book is that among the shared grievances fostering the violent radicalization movement was the humiliation that its future participants suffered under the tortuous practices of the state. This humiliation represents a particular culturally constructed emotional experience rooted in the state's violations of religious, social, and cultural values and understandings. It is one that is not necessarily generalizable to all social movements, which may exhibit shared grievances of a different nature and with different effects on commitment to engage in collective action (e.g., radical collective action that entails the use of extremely violent tactics). That is, shared grievances are culturally and socially grounded in certain kinds of emotions that can shape the conditions under which some participants otherwise committed to peaceful protest tactics might be mobilized to engage in violent tactics. I conclude, therefore, that although shared grievances are not alone enough to explain the emergence of social movements, we should treat shared grievances as an important variable rather than as a constant.
2. Additionally, some social movement scholars have argued that the state's repression can prevent social movements from emerging or can contribute to their decline after they have emerged. Indeed, this has been a central tenet of both the resource mobilization and political process theories. Others, drawing upon state constructionist approaches, have shown that the state's violent indiscriminate repression can instead serve to further fuel social movement emergence and/or ongoing activity (see, e.g., Walton 1984;

Goldstone 1989; Brockett 1993; Goodwin 2003; Dale 2011; Kurtz and Smithey 2008; Hafez 2003). Using examples and empirical data from several social movements, scholars have demonstrated that such repressive practices, meant to demobilize a social movement, rebellion, or social revolution, can be counterproductive and lead to unintended outcomes. This is a condition often referred to as the *"paradox of repression."* (Kurtz and Smithey 2008)

In Egypt, this *paradox of repression* created an immense desire in young individuals to fight back and take justice into their own hands. Repressed activists were clouded by rage and supported by powerful cultural narratives to justify their use of violence. As a result, the once nonviolent protesters found their way to organizing revolutionary violent militias, in order to attain some sort of social change and vigilante justice. But there is another dynamic as well that it concealed within this interpretation of the paradox of repression. In this book I have demonstrated a case that yields additional insight into the effects of state repression on social movements. Even when the state's use of violent repression is not indiscriminate, but rather focused (through selective and intentionally targeted incidents of torture) and "justified" by the state, this can not only further fuel the social movement that the state is targeting, but—at least under conditions when those targeted directly by the state's violence perceive it as "unjustified" and "humiliating" (or otherwise mediated by deeply constructed emotions)—it can transform the commitments of movement participants. In some cases even leading them to engage in violent tactics that they were previously unwilling to adopt in their pursuit of justice. Indeed, it can reframe what some of the movement's participants subsequently understand as their pursuit of justice to mean.

The state-sponsored torture and rampant abuses by security officers and interrogators were designed to generate a sense of shame and humiliation to many, once proud, young activists. "They beat me until I say (*ana mara*)," said Ramy. This phrase translates as "I am a female"—a culturally humiliating way to shame a proud man and depict him as a weak and submissive person.

Khaled, a twenty-nine-year-old activist detained between 2014–2016, told Human Rights Watch in a report published in 2017, "You're at their mercy, 'Whatever we say, you're going to do.' They electrocuted me in my head, testicles, under my armpits. They used to heat water and throw it on you. Every time I lost consciousness; they would throw it on me."

When state institutions practiced systematic techniques of physical and psychological torture—that humiliated and shamed victims—the legitimacy of the state was undermined. Once the legitimacy of the state was undermined, and the trust in state institutions broken, the activists I interviewed no longer saw the state as the only actor with agency over the "legitimate use of physical force"—in other words, as said in one interview, "[the Egyptian police] is not a legitimate and professional force. These are gangs in uniform, the only difference is that they have weapons and call themselves a state entity. If they want war, then let it be."[1]

The widespread repressive practices and methods of torture—that were primarily aimed at undermining the activists' will and commitment to resistance—went too far. Their methods of repression targeted and intentionally violated deep cultural and religious values that invoked profound emotions of humiliation, which fueled a radical transformation in their perspective on what tactics are and are not permissible in the pursuit of justice. The states' particular form of repression not only fueled the movement's challenge to the state but contributed to the movement's use and escalation of violence in doing so.

3. The absence, and in some cases the inefficiency, of nonviolent channels and means to protest government policies, could push activists to radical thinking, and to change the status quo.

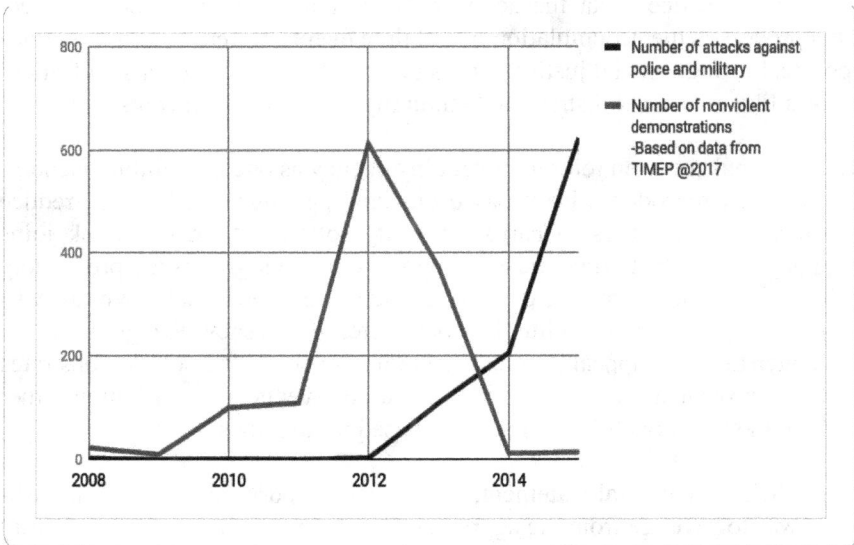

Figure 4.1.   Violent vs. nonviolent activity from 2008–2015 in Egypt based on data from TIMEP@2017

The illustration in (Figure 4.1)[2] shows the inverse relationship between violence and freedom of expression in Egypt. In the period between 2008–2013, Egypt witnessed some moderate political reforms which resulted in an opening in the public space and allowed for social movements to organize activities and mobilize supporters. In this period, there was a minimal violent activity in Egypt, with exception to a few attacks inside the Sinai Peninsula on the gas pipes that run from Egypt to Israel and Jordan, and one larger attack in Alexandria on January 7, 2011.

In contrast, in the period between 2013 and 2015, the opposite happened. A massive state-led crackdown on social movements and nonviolent protesters resulted in closure of the public sphere (Hamzawy 2017). Local and international human rights watchdogs estimated as many as 60,000 were detained on politically motivated charges and had no chance of fair trial proceedings (at the end of Mubarak's rule, the figure was approximately 5,000). The issuance of law 107/2013 0-, which banned all demonstrations, effectively outlawed the majority of social movements in Egypt and left no channels for nonviolent expression of discontent. This same period witnessed an unprecedented influx of insurgents and violent attacks on state, police, and military facilities.

Egypt's latest wave of violent radicalization thus can be understood as largely reactive, not proactive. It is a multifaceted process that includes a series of extraordinary—and often traumatizing—events that motivate a turn to violent behavior. The violent behavior is seen as a last resort, and a means to an end—justice—that the actors believe cannot otherwise be achieved. This process is the accumulation of multiple events driven by grand motives (political change, social justice, etc.) and is further enabled by a set of micro factors like emotional distress and culturally constructed concepts.

4. Policymakers often refer to violent insurgency as one monolithic phenomenon that reproduces itself based on fixed paradigms or, at best, reduce the countermeasures to narrow security solutions. But this book joins many studies that argue the exact opposite: violent groups are profoundly diverse in their motives, objectives, tactics, and end-goals. We are witnessing a new era of culturally constructed insurgency. Religions are no longer the only appealing recruitment approach. This book demonstrates how newer insurgents in Egypt focused on revenge and retribution rather than the traditional jihadi, religious-based motivations.

Ajnad Misr's inaugural statement, stated that the purpose of their establishment was to "avenge from the aggressors."[3] "We are targeting senior security officers who were involved in the violent dispersal of the Rab'a sit-in, in order to retaliate for our proud women who were captured by the state."[4] The first video released of the group similarly emphasized a revenge narrative, rather than a jihadi discourse. *Retribution Is Life* video repeatedly showed several scenes of police officers assaulting nonviolent demonstrators in multiple instances—each of those scenes was followed by a stern respond from Ajnad Misr members to avenge for the "innocent citizens" assaulted by the police. The whole video was then dedicated to the mothers who lost their sons and daughters in police violence.

5. The role of ideology in the formation or creation of the post-2013 insurgency seems to be diminishing in deference to other factors. It is merely a pragmatic element or a convenient mobilization tactic to tie a cause to religious grounds. Unlike Al-Qaeda and the Islamic State where ideology plays a key role in their recruitment and public discourse, ideology was more malleable for Egypt's nascent domestic insurgency. Through their public statements, interviews, and other accounts, we understand that ideology was neither motive nor a factor in its sustainability. Instead of posing themselves as religious warriors or advocates of an Islamic Caliphate, we find that insurgents depict themselves as vigilante justice seekers who are fighting against tyrannical rule of the military generals.

Future Research

The findings of this study contribute to current literature: first, by providing answers to the question of the radical transformation in post-2013 Egypt; and, second, by challenging the existing literature and traditional theories that overlook potent factors that contribute to the creation of violent insurgency.

Without the rare insight into a group of insurgents, it would have been very difficult to fully grasp the impact of the traumatic and emotionally demeaning events that these activists experienced during the course of transformation. This transformation may have been jarring in one isolated case, but the sheer number of young individuals converting to violent tactics revealed a burgeoning movement.

This terrifying, and rapidly growing, phenomenon warrants additional study. It is important to continue the research efforts beyond traditional paradigms and modalities, and to further explore this period of violent insurgency in Egypt and elsewhere. Scholars should be open and willing to reconsider postulates about violent insurgents and armed militias. The traditional profile of violent insurgent as a random by-product of poverty or lack of education is no longer commonsensical, if ever it was (Magouirk, Atran, and Sageman 2008).

The aforementioned groups involved many highly educated people whose intelligence helped them utilize online communication technologies to convey their messages, document their attacks, and enhance their recruiting efforts.

This book leaves us with more questions to answer in the future, but also suggests a methodological model to apply in research related to violent insurgent movements. This field would benefit from more direct, localized studies where the researchers can gather the necessary data to facilitate micro-social process analysis. Living the research experience, and fully appreciating the cultural context that governs the activists' responses and behaviors, provides the needed background for researchers to recognize the various factors at play in these social movements. This can drastically alter the way we understand radicalization, and more importantly, how we develop strategies for reversing it.

While I believe that the conclusions drawn in this book would be very useful in studying similar cases, it is important to highlight that this model faces a limitation to the extent that we might generalize its conclusions, especially in different cultural contexts. Relying on emotions that are deeply engrained in cultural and social codes, like humiliation, pride, shame, and outrage, makes my conclusions plausible to other cases in an Egyptian and Middle Eastern environment. However, in order to make valuable use of this study in different cultural environments, a researcher must pay close attention to the local cultural and subcultural codes and concepts when analyzing their data. For example, this study focuses on *humiliation*—and its role in constructing a social sense of *shame,* that drives outrage and ultimately leads to radical transformation, yet the triggers of *humiliation* vary dramatically from one culture to another, and thus, the associated feelings of shame and pride could lead to different results and outcomes.

Further attention to such contexts would also require considering how culturally constructed feelings like revenge might be differently mediated by socioeconomic differences, and consider how revenge in particular, which has long been invoked by diverse Egyptian social movements, is differently generated, articulated, appropriated, and practiced across a variety of movement contexts.

On Deradicalization

Although this project is focused on violent radicalization and not deradicalization, the research showed that radicalization is a dynamic and multi-layered process and suggests that so must be the efforts to reverse it. Deradicalization should reflect a deep understanding of the accumulated motives that led to violence in first place. The root causes and grievances that initially led to radicalization must be addressed directly in order to reverse it, but reversal is possible (Horgan 2008, Qazi 2011; Azam and Fatima 2017) and should be preferred to lethal crackdowns and violent countermeasures against violent actors (which could further the ripple effect of radicalization).

This study also further emphasizes, as many scholars have confirmed, that radicalization should not be oversimplified and characterized as strictly a security problem. Many governments around the world have been trying to counter insurgency with very little success. If F-16s and Hellfire missiles were effective deterrents against insurgents, then the United States should have been able to deter Al-Qaeda many years ago. We should have not witnessed the growing number of insurgents that have emerged since the 1980s. The "security solutions" that included regular attacks did nothing but strengthen the commitment of militants to their cause.

In a phone interview with an inactive (retired) insurgent, who now lives outside Egypt, I was told he quit violent insurgency after he managed to take the revenge he sought from his suspected assailant in 2014. "I have achieved what I wanted, and it makes me feel at peace." He didn't want to reveal any information regarding the attack he was allegedly involved in, but he emphasized that his sole intent to join such groups was to take revenge from the person who tortured him—when he accomplished it, he quit. Had the assailant been held accountable, and justice served through lawful means, it would have been unlikely that this person would have joined insurgent groups in the first place.

Containing violent movements will be a long and multifaceted effort. In a globalized and increasingly interconnected world, one government, no matter how powerful, cannot initiate and sustain a deradicalization effort on its own without the support of local communities, intergovernmental agencies, NGOs, and above all, a strong political will to end support to tyrannical regimes.

Closing Remarks

Far more than just an academic pursuit that researches a complex time in Egypt's modern history, this book presents the stories, ideas, experiences, and other social processes that influenced activists as they experienced the radical evolution from passionate nonviolent activism to violent insurgency. These are the memories of life-defining moments and painful experiences.

As an Egyptian nonviolent activist, myself, I have shared the feeling of incredible triumph at moments of revolutionary success and the crushing defeat that ends our thriving hope. I have lived the experience of a dying dream. At the outset, our aims were simple—basic human rights respected by the state and participation in the system that is nurtured and valued. Our means were nonviolent, and our hopes were limitless.

We believed in the revolutionary struggles of history that demonstrated the success of nonviolent movements. We studied the teachings, and we absorbed the richness of the experiences and the words of those who came before us. We knew it would not be easy, but we knew a nonviolent revolution was the only way to achieve what had always been beyond reach for the people of modern Egypt.

Our dreams were, however, short-lived. Three years of tumultuous transition ended with a military coup d'état and the implementation of exceptional measures that led the country to fall into an extremely polarized and congested political atmosphere. The ultimate effect was the restoration of tyrannical practices on a wider and more violent scale than those witnessed under former President Mubarak's rule. With public space being closed, pro-democracy movements outlawed, and the judiciary being co-opted by the military, the chance for social change, protest, or democratization, let alone for holding military or police officers accountable for their violations, became impossible.

When failures started to mount, and the promise of our future became increasingly bleak our dreams began to fade. From the depths of our being, we yearned for basic freedom and protections from violations against us at the hand of the state. For some, the flickering hope began to inspire fantasies of violence, if violence was the only available way to attain our ultimate goal. The means of achieving success no longer mattered as much as the success itself. Many nonviolent activists began drifting toward violent militias and called for taking up arms against the state.

Grave humiliation, achieved by horrific torture at the hands of the state, has the capacity to transform the most peaceful protestor into a reluctant radical. The fervor with which that radical will pursue revenge is limitless. While many of us started as nonviolent protesters decades ago in pursuit of democratic changes and have lived together through the rise and fall of our dream, few of us have experienced the particularly cruel level of state-sponsored violence that led to a search for alternative methods of achieving justice. As people, our ability to empathize with one another is critical to our ability to understand social movements. Through the stories told here, it becomes clear that the fathers, sons, lovers, brothers, students, and professionals that made up the 2013 wave of insurgency are not fundamentally unlike us or inherently unhinged.

Examples like Ramy, Hussein, Tarek, and others, who all started as nonviolent protesters, transformed into violent militants after experiencing first-hand traumatic events, like torture, abuse, and losing beloved family members. Violent insurgency became a magnet for frustrated, defeated nonviolent protesters who experienced years of failure and relentless rebukes from the state. Violence was neither a first choice nor was it driven by ideology or religion for many young, radicalized activists. Most of those militants were side by side with us throughout the January 2011 revolution, where one of the main chants was "we are peaceful," but they decided to switch tactics only after 2013's military coup d'état.

Resorting to violent tactics came when they could not resolve their grievances through legal and constitutional means. And even then, only when they were humiliated and stripped of their most basic human rights. The transformation came after the torture that eliminated their ability to believe any longer in the promise that the Egyptian state could be changed through nonviolent tactics. The state intentionally sought to humiliate these men through the use of coercive tactics. In doing so, the state achieved a transformation of their citizen-subjects' psyches. Ironically, and tragically, the state transformed these once committed nonviolent protesters into violent militants—citizens willing to use the very same forms of violence that the state had used against them.

Although some embers of the revolution may still burn discreetly in Egypt, those who lived through the rise and fall of the Arab Spring share a unique bond by living the shared experience, despite the different routes we chose as our methods of expression and resistance.

NOTES

1. The subject didn't want to be named.
2. Data was collected from the security watch program by Tahrir Institute for Middle East Policy. The project relies on statements and media published on the accounts of terror actors themselves. Access to these statements was obtained through monitoring of jihadi web forums and terror groups' social media pages.

In determining which events to record, the project tracks only those events which could reasonably be considered acts of "terrorism" or the state's proclaimed response to such acts. Yet, "terrorism" and "terrorist" are themselves heavily contested terms. Thus, in order to capture the current threat faced by Egypt, this project adopts a definition of "terror attack" as one that entails premeditated violence carried out for political ends. This does not include the threat of attack, but rather only executed violence. Political ends may be defined as any which have a reasonable bearing on changing an established power dynamic. For this reason, premeditated targeting of religious institutions where it could be reasonably assumed that these were targeted in their political nature are included; however, religious institutions or religious minority civilians targeted as a result of local conflict are not included (although these are documented in TIMEP's Eshhad project).

3. Ajnad Misr Statement Number 1, January 2014.
4. Ajnad Misr Statement Number 5, April 2014.

References

Abdel Azim, Ahmed. 2014. Egypt's Supreme Council of Armed Forces—SCAF delegates Field Marshal Abdel Fattah El Sisi to run for President. Arabic *Al Watan News*. https://www.elwatannews.com/news/details/405796.

Abdel Moneim, Intisar. 2011. *Diaries of a Former Sister: My Stories with The Muslim Brotherhood.* General Egyptian Book Organization.

Abou El Fadl, Khaled. 2007. *The Great Theft: Wrestling Islam from the Extremists.* Harper Collins: Reprint edition (2007). p. 227.

"A bulldozer bulldozes dozens of the bodies of the victims of the fourth massacre." 2013b. YouTube Video, 0:47. Posted by "Aljazeera Channel." August 26, 2013. https://www.youtube.com/watch?v=EJ2y1meVy6U.

Adler, Alfred. 1956. *The Individual Psychology of Alfred Adler* 1. New York, NY: Basic Books.

AFP. 2013. "Egypt Designates Muslim Brotherhood as a Terrorist Organization." *France 24*. December 25, 2016. https://www.france24.com/ar/20131225-8.

Agencies. 2010. "The Forensic Report on the Re-Autopsy of Khaled Saeed Shows That He Died from Suffocation Asphyxia." *Al-Dustour News*, June 23, 2010. https://web.archive.org/web/20100628031728/http://dostor.org/politics/egypt/10/june/23/20155?quicktabs_1=2

Aḥmad Abū Zayd. 1965. "al-Thaʾr: dirāsah anthrūpūlūjiyyah bi-iḥdā qurā al-saʿīd." Cairo: Dār al-Maʿārif.

"Ahmed Moussa gets excited on the air: 'Who allowed this shame to be presented and distributed in Egypt?' On my responsibility" 2018. YouTube Video, 0:40. By Sada Elbalad, February 28, 2018. https://www.youtube.com/watch?v=2bG8zghmi4c.

"Ajnad Misr fifth communique." 2014. YouTube video. Posted by "Al Qasas Hayat." January 3, 2014.

"Ajnad Misr first video communique." 2014. YouTube video. Posted by "Al Qasas Hayat." January 3, 2014. https://www.youtube.com/watch?v=mmJ-AU4nn3U.

"Ajnad Misr fourth communique." 2014. YouTube video. Posted by "Al Qasas Hayat." January 3, 2014.

"Ajnad Misr second video communique." 2014. YouTube video. Posted by "Al Qasas Hayat." January 3, 2014.

"Ajnad Misr sixth communique." 2014. YouTube video. Posted by "Al Qasas Hayat." January 3, 2014.

"Ajnad Misr third video communique." 2014. YouTube video. Posted by "Al Qasas Hayat." January 3, 2014.

"Ajnad Misr video confessions during police interrogation." 2014. YouTube video. Posted by "Al Qasas Hayat." January 3, 2014.

Akhbar Al-youm Media report. 2013. "Muslim Brotherhood Exploits the Poor." *Akhbar Al-youm News*. August 17, 2013.

Al-Ahram Center. 2006. *Economic and Social Alterations in the Egyptian Society 1*. Cairo: Ahram Press.

———. 2009. *Economic and Social Alterations in the Egyptian Society 71*. Cairo: Ahram Press.

Al Ahram Online. 2013a. "Egypt Military Unveils Transitional Roadmap." *Al-Ahram News*, July 3, 2013. https://english.ahram.org.eg/News/75631.aspx.

———. 2013b. "Official Statement of Egypt's Minister of Interior regarding Rab'aa Sit-in dispersal." *Al-Ahram News*, August 14, 2013. http://gate.ahram.org.eg /News/383155.aspx

———. 2013c. "15 dead, 134 injured in Egypt's Mansoura explosion." *Al-Ahram News*, December 14, 2013. https://english.ahram.org.eg/News/89902.aspx.

———. 2013d. "A Reading in the New Governors' Appointments . . . Generals from the Military, Police, Absence of Religious Currents and the Return of Mubarak Allies." *Al-Ahram News,* August 8, 2013. http://gate.ahram.org.eg/News/382293 .aspx.

"Al-Arian's wife kisses his hands after the judge allows her to see him." 2016. YouTube video, 3:54. Posted by "ElWatan News." August 9, 2016. https://www .youtube.com/watch?v=l_cCVcpO8Eo.

"Alashmawy Hisham's video statement speaking on his decision to split from Anas Bait Al Makdas." 2020. YouTube video, February 1, 2020. https://www.youtube .com/watch?v=AbnHvU.

Al Jazeera TV. 2013 "Beyond the News." *Al Jazeera News*, April 21, 2013.

Al Jazeera News. 2016. "Massacre in Rabaa: Three Years on, Egyptians Reflect on the Worst Attack on Protesters in Modern History." *Al Jazeera News*, August 17, 2016. https://www.aljazeera.com/program/episode/2016/8/17/massacre-in-rabaa.

Al Jazeera News. 2014. "Egyptian detainees 'tortured and raped.'" *Al Jazeera News*. April 1, 2014. https://www.aljazeera.com/humanrights/2014/04/egyptian-detainees -tortured-raped-201441165823978172.html.

Al Jazeera. 2013. "Egypt declares state of emergency." Aljazeera, News Agencies, July 4, 2013. https://www.aljazeera.com/news/middleeast/2013/08/201381413509 551214html.

Al Kwakbi, Abdel Rahaman. 1902. *Taba'e Al Estebdad w Masa'er Al Ebad*. Cairo: Dar El Maaref Press.

Allam, Mona. 2012. "Women in the Muslim Brotherhood: A follower or equal?" *Al Safeer Al Araby*. October 10, 2012.

Allen-Collinson, Jacquelyn, and Helen Owton. 2014. "Take a deep breath: Asthma, sporting embodiment, the senses and 'auditory work.'" *International review for the sociology of sport* 49 (5): 592–608. https://journals.sagepub.com/doi/abs /10.1177/1012690212463918.

Allen, Charles E. 2010. *De-radicalizing Islamist Extremists.* RAND Corp Arlington, VA: National Security Research Division.

Allen, Johnie J., Craig A. Anderson, and Brad J. Bushman. 2018. "The General Aggression Model." *Current Opinion in Psychology* 22: 96–96. Elsevier B.V. https:// doi.org/10.1016/j.copsyc.2017.03.034.

Al Watan News Arabic. 2015. "Islamic Group's Leader Dies in Cairo's Prison." *Al Watan News.* August 10, 2015. https://bit.ly/3qWAXiu.

Aman, Ayah. 2014. "Female Prisoners in Egypt Suffer Rampant Abuse." *Egypt Pulse* 30. https://www.al-monitor.com/pulse/originals/2014/06/egypt-female -detainees-abuse-harassment-prison.html.

Amin, Ash. 2004. "Regulating Economic Globalization." *Transactions of the Institute of British Geographers* 29 (2): 217–233.

Amin, Galal. 2005. *Whatever Happened to Egyptian: Phase Three.* Cairo: AUC press.

Amnesty. 2012. "Agents of Repression: Egypt's Police and the Case for Reform." *Amnesty International,* October 12, 2012. https://www.amnesty.org/download /Documents/24000/mde120292012en.pdf.

Anderson, Sulomen. 2016. "Terrorist to the World, Hero at Home: The Legacy of Hezbollah's Dead Military Commander." *VICE News,* May 18, 2016. https://www .vice.com/en/article/mbnw3x/terrorist-to-the-world-hero-at-home-the-legacy-of -hezbollahs-dead-military-commander.

"An interview with Gen. Ibrahim, Director of Scorpio Prison." 2012. YouTube video. Posted by "Al Hayat TV." https://www.youtube.com/watch?v=DQuQisEhO80.

"An open dialogue with the chief officer of Ajnad Misr." 2014. YouTube video, Recorded interview with Hamam Attia (Magd el din El-Masry). Video Statement. 2014. https://www.youtube.com/watch?v=kmvHReRX05U.

Apter, David E. 1997. "Political violence in analytical perspective." *The legitimization of Violence* 1: 1–32. London, UK: Palgrave Macmillan.

Ashour, Mohamed. 2013. "Interview with Mohamed Morsi, the MB elections coordinator during 2010 election." *Al Watan News.* June 26, 2013. https://www.elwatan news.com/news/details/210757

Atran, Scott. 2003. "Genesis of suicide terrorism." *Science* 299 (5612): 1534–1539. https://science.sciencemag.org/content/299/5612/1534/tab-article-info.

Ayyash, Abdelrahman. 2019. "Strong Organization, Weak Ideology: Muslim Brotherhood Trajectories in Egyptian Prisons Since 2013." *Arab Reform Initiative,* April 29, 2019.

Azam, Zubair, and Syeda Bareeha Fatima. 2017. "Mishal: a case study of a deradicalization and emancipation program in Swat Valley, Pakistan." *Journal for Deradicalization* 11: 1–29.

Azhar, Mobeen. 2014. "The School That Says Osama Bin Laden Was a Hero." *BBC World Service,* Islamabad. November 11, 2014. https://www.bbc.com/news/maga zine-30005278.

Baldwin, Clive, Andrew Mawson, Bill Frelick, and Heba Morayef. 2009. "Service for Life: State Repression and Indefinite Conscription in Eritrea." *Human Rights Watch Report.* https://www.hrw.org/report/2009/04/16/service-life/state-repression-and-indefinite-conscription-eritrea.

Bandura, Albert. 1999. "Moral disengagement in the perpetration of inhumanities." *Personality and Social Psychology Review* 3 (3): 193–209.

Başoğlu, Metin, Maria Livanou, Cvetana Crnobarić, Tanja Frančišković, Enra Suljić, Dijana Đurić, and Melin Vranešić. 2005. "Psychiatric and cognitive effects of war in former Yugoslavia: Association of lack of redress for trauma and posttraumatic stress reactions." *Jama* 294 (5): 580–590. https://doi.org/10.1001/jama.294.5.580.

"Battle of Revenge for the Muslims of Egypt #3: Targeting Military Intelligence in al–Ismāʿīlīyah." 2014. Internet Archive video message. Posted by "Jamāʾat Anṣār Bayt al–Maqdis." https://archive.org/details/mail41563gd.

BBC, 2014a. "An Egyptian Court Sentence 528 MB members to death." *BBC News,* Arabic. https://www.bbc.com/arabic/middleeast/2014/03/140324_egypt_trials_mutfi.

———. 2016. "Egyptian four-year-old's life sentence a mistake, military says." *BBC News,* Arabic. February 22, 2016. https://www.bbc.com/news/world–middle–east–35633314.

———. 2014b. "Saudi Arabia Declares MB, Hezbullah, and ISIL, as Terrorist Organizations." *BBC News,* Arabic, March 7, 2014. https://www.bbc.com/arabic/middleeast/2014/03/140307_saudi_terror_organizations.

———. 2007. "Emad El Kbeer's Assailant Officer Sentenced to 3 years." *BBC Arabic.com,* July 14, 2007. http://news.bbc.co.uk/hi/arabic/middle_east_news/newsid_7079000/7079123.stm.

Beck, Ulrich. 2013. "Toward a new critical theory with a cosmopolitan intent." *Constellations* 10 (4): 453–468.

Ben-Yehuda, Nachman. 2012. *Political Assassinations by Jews: A Rhetorical Device for Justice.* SUNY Press.

Bondokji, Neven, Kim Wilkinson, and Leen Aghabi. 2017. "Understanding adicalisation: A Literature Review of Models and Drivers." *Aman: WANA Institute.*

Borum, Randy. 2011a. "Radicalization into Violent Extremism I: A Review of Social Science Theories." *Journal of Strategic Security* 4: 9.

———. 2011b. "Radicalization into Violent Extremism II: A Review of Conceptual Models and Empirical Research," *Journal of Strategic Security* 4: 41–42.

Brackenridge, C. 1999. "Managing Myself: Investigator Survival in Sensitive Research." *International Review for the Sociology of Sport* 34 (4): 399–410.

Bradfield, Murray, and Karl Aquino. 1999. "The effects of blame attributions and offender likableness on forgiveness and revenge in the workplace." *Journal of Management* 25 (5): 607–631.

Brockett, Charles D. 1993. "A Protest–Cycle Resolution of the Repression/Popular Protest Paradox." *Social Science History* 17 (3): 457–484.

Burke, Jason. 2004. "Secret world of US jails". *The Observer U.K.* London, June 12, 2004. https://waynenorthey.com/wp–content/uploads/2015/03/Secret-World-of-US-Jails.pdf.

C. Williams, Amanda C. de, and Jannie van der Merwe. 2013. "The Psychological Impact of Torture." *British Journal of Pain* 7 (2): 101–106. https://doi.org/10.1177/2049463713483596.

Calhoun, Craig. 2001. "Putting emotions in their place." *Passionate politics: Emotions and social movements.* 1: 45–57. University of Chicago Press.

Caren, Neal. 2007. "Political process theory." *The Blackwell Encyclopedia of Sociology*, February 15, 2007. https://doi.org/10.1002/9781405165518.wbeosp041.

Castells, Manuel. 2009. *The Rise of the Network Society: The Information Age: Economy, Society, and Culture* 2 (1). Wiley-Blackwell.

———. 2012. *Networks of Outrage and Hope: Social Movements in the Internet Age.* Malden, MA: Polity Press.

Chenoweth, Erica, and Maria J. Stephan. 2011. *Why civil resistance works: The strategic logic of nonviolent conflict.* Columbia University Press.

Chomsky, Noam. 2011. "On Libya and the Unfolding *Crises."* An interview with *Stephen Shalom and Michael Albert, Znet* 31 (3).

Collins, Randall. 1975. *Conflict sociology.* New York: Academic Press.

———. 2008. *Violence: A micro–sociological theory.* Princeton University Press.

"Confessions of the members of the first terrorist cell." 2014. YouTube video, 3:51. Posted by "Moiegy." May 12, 2014. https://www.youtube.com/watch?v=r6Oqam DxyUw&list=UUWUJwemS3xkwrpkW80vQcFg.

Cooley, Charles Horton. 1922. "Chapter 5—The Social Self-1. The Meaning of I." *Human Nature and the Social Order.* New York: Charles Scribner's Sons, (1922): 168–210.

Coolsaet, Rik. 2016. "Facing the fourth foreign fighters' wave: what drives Europeans to Syria, and to IS? Insights from the Belgian case." *Egmont Paper* 81.

Cook, Steven A. 2007. *Ruling but not governing: The military and political development in Egypt, Algeria, and Turkey.* JHU Press.

Crossett, Chuck, and Jason Spitaleta, 2010. *Radicalization: Relevant Psychological and Sociological Concepts.* Johns Hopkins University.

Crenshaw, Martha. 1981. "The causes of terrorism." *Comparative politics* 13 (4): 379–399.

Dale, John. 2008. "Burma's Boomerang: Human Rights, Social Movements and Transnational Legal Mechanisms 'from below." *International Journal of Contemporary Sociology* 45 (1): 151–184.

Dale, John G. 2011. *Free Burma: Transnational Legal Action and Corporate Accountability.* Minneapolis: University of Minnesota Press.

Davidson, Jacob. 2015. "Here's how many internet users there are." *Time Magazine.* https://time.com/3896219/internet-users-worldwide/.

Deutsche Welle News. 2011. "Egyptian Officer: 'Virginity Tests for Demonstrators to Prevent Rape Charges.'" *Deutsche Welle News*, June 27, 2011. https://p.dw.com/p/11k7Y.

———. 2014. "Egyptian satirist Bassem Youssef stops show, fearing for safety." *Deutsche Welle News*, June 3, 2014. https://www.dw.com/en/egyptian-satirist-bassem-youssef-stops-show-fearing-for-safety/a-17678157.

————. 2013. "Muslim Brotherhood Refuses Sisi's Threats." *Deutsche Welle News,* July 24, 2013. https://www.dw.com/ar/16973492.

"Dr. Ali Jumaa: The Muslim Brotherhood is the basis of black terrorism." 2015. YouTube video, 12:03. Recorded from a TV Interview on CBC Channel. Posted by "CBC Egypt." July 27, 2015. https://www.youtube.com/watch?v=HHwUw5JbD-0&t=501s.

Douglas, Kitrina, and David Carless. 2012. "Membership, Golf and a Story about Anna and Me: Reflections on Research in Elite Sport." *Qualitative Methods in Psychology Bulletin, Sports and Performance* 1 (13): 27–35.

————. 2013. "An invitation to performative research." *Methodological innovations online* 8 (1): 53–64. https://doi.org/10.4256/mio.2013.0004.

Du Bois, W. E. B. 1903. *The Souls of Black Folk.* 196–197. New York: Bantam Classic.

————. 1994.*The Souls of Black Folk.* 196–197. New York: Bantam Classic.

Durkheim, Emile. 1995. *The Elementary forms of the religious life.* translated by Karen E. Fields. New York: Free Press.

Egypt State Report. 2016. *Baseera Center.* Cairo. http://baseera.com.eg/AR/Reports2.aspx?ID=246.

Egyptian Constitutional Declaration. 2012. "English text of Morsi's Constitutional Declaration." *Ahram Online,* November 22, 2012. http://english.ahram.org.eg/News/58947.aspx.

"Egyptian Election Commission." 2011. Official Site: National Election Authority. https://www.elections.eg/en/.

El Ansary, Mohamed. 2017. "The Role of the Public Prosecution in Egypt's Repression."

El Badry, Youssry, Essam Abo Sadira, Nabil Abo Shal, and Ali Shawky. 2014. "Dabaa Check Point Attack." *Al Masry Al Youm News.* June 5, 2014. https://www.almasryalyoum.com/news/details/495603.

El Masry, Tarek. 2013. "A state of calm in the sit–in in Damietta Clock Square after the remnants incited against the Socialist Revolutionaries." *El-Eshtraki: Media for Revolution.* July 3, 2013.

El–Sayed, Jehad. 2018. "Military court sentences Iskandarani to 10 years in prison." *Egypt Today*, May 22, 2018. https://www.egypttoday.com/Article/1/50656/Military-court-sentences-Iskandarani-to-10-years-in-prison.

El Sayed, Samar. 2019. "Poverty Rate in Urban Upper Egypt Decreases for the First Time" *Al-mal News.*

Elster, Jon. 1990. "Norms of Revenge." *Ethics* 100 (4): 862–885. https://www.jstor.org/stable/2381783.

Emerson, Michael O., and David Hartman. 2006. "The rise of religious fundamental-ism." *Annu. Rev. Sociol.* 32: 127–144.

Essa, Ibrahim. 2009. *Mubarak Wa'asru Wamasru.* Cairo: Madboli Press.

Fahim, Kareem. 2013. "Egypt, dealing a blow to the Muslim brotherhood, deems it a terrorist group." *The New York Times.* December 5, 2013. https://www.nytimes.com/2013/12/26/world/middleeast/egypt-calls-muslim-brotherhood-a-terrorist-group.html.

Fahim, Kareem, and El Sheikh, Mayy. 2013. "Egyptian Officials Point at Islamist Group After Blast at Police Building." *The New York Times*, December 24, 2013. https://www.nytimes.com/2013/12/25/world/middleeast/egypt-car-bomb.html.

Fahmy, Khaled. 2000. *All the Pasha's Men Mehmed Ali, his Army and the Making of Modern Egypt* 1. Cambridge Middle East Studies.

———. 2005. "Dissecting the modern Egyptian state." *International Journal of Middle East Studies* 47 (3): 559–562.

Fahmy, Nabil. 2013. General Assembly of the United Nations General Debate. https://gadebate.un.org/en/68/egypt.

"First media release by Ajnad Misr." 2014. YouTube video. Posted by "Al Qasas Hayat." https://www.youtube.com/watch?v=mmJ-AU4nn3U.

Fischman, Yael. 1991. "Interacting with trauma: Clinicians' responses to treating psychological aftereffects of political repression." *American Journal of Orthopsychiatry* 61(2): 179–185. https://doi.org/10.1037/h0079247.

Fitzgibbons, Richard P. 1986. "The cognitive and emotive uses of forgiveness in the treatment of anger." *Psychotherapy: Theory, Research, Practice, Training*, 23 (4): 629–633.

Foran, John. 2005. *Taking power: On the origins of third world revolutions*. Cambridge University Press.

Fouda, Yosri. 2017. "Investigative documentary on weapons trafficking in North Africa." *DW made for minds*, September 22, 2019.

Fredrickson, Barbara L. 2009. "Why Choose Hope?" *Psychology Today*. March 23, 2009. https://www.psychologytoday.com/us/blog/positivity/200903/why-choose-hope.

Galtung, Johan. 1969. "Violence, Peace, and Peace Research." *Journal of Peace Research* 6 (3): 167–191.

Ganguly, Meenakshi. 2001. "A banking system built for terrorism." *Time Magazine* 5. October 5, 2001. http://content.time.com/time/world/article/0,8599,178227,00.html.

Ghonim, Wael. 2012. *Revolution 2.0: The Power of the People Is Greater Than the People in Power, A Memoir*. Houghton Mifflin Harcourt.

Giddens, Anthony. 1990. *The Consequences of Modernity*. Stanford: Stanford University Press.

Gille, Zsuzsa, and Seán Ó. Riain. 2002. "Global Ethnography." *Annual Review of Sociology* 28 (1): 271–295.

Gilligan, James. 2003. "Shame, guilt, and violence." *Social Research: An International Quarterly* 70 (4): 1149–1180.

Ginges, Jeremy, and Scott Atran. 2008. "Humiliation and the inertia effect: Implications for understanding violence and compromise in intractable intergroup conflicts." *Journal of Cognition and Culture* 8 (3–4): 281–294. http://dx.doi.org.mutex.gmu.edu/10.1163/156853708X358182.

Girard, René. 2007. *Violence and the Sacred*. Duke University Press.

Girisha Ali, Zibiq Sherif Mohamed. 1979. "Asalyib Alghazw Alfikry Lel Alem AlIslami." *Wafa*. Saudi Arabia: Dar El E'esam Publishers.

Global Terrorism Database, University of Maryland. http://www.start.umd.edu/gtd
/Press.

Goffman, Erving. 1967. *Interaction ritual: Essays on face–to–face Behavior.* New
York: Anchor Books.

———. 1974. *Frame Analysis.* New York: Harper & Row.

Goldstein, Robert J. 1978. *Political repression in modern America: From 1870 to the
present.* Boston: G.K. Hall.

Goldstone, Jack Andrew. 1989. "Deterrence in rebellions and revolutions." In *Perspectives on Deterrence.* P. Stern, R. Axelrod, R. Jervis, and R. Radner, eds. New
York: Oxford University Press.

———. 2014. *Revolutions: A Very Short Introduction.* Oxford: Oxford University
Press.

Goodwin, Jeff. 2003. "State-centered approaches to social revolutions." *Theorizing
Revolutions* 11: 9–35. https://nyuscholars.nyu.edu/en/publications/state-centered
-approaches-to-social-revolutions-strengths-and-lim.

Goodwin, Jeff, James M. Jasper, and Francesca Polletta. 2001. *Passionate politics:
Emotions and social movements.* University of Chicago Press. https://doi.org
/10.1007/978–0–387–30715–2_27.

Gotowicki, Stephen H. 1997. "The role of the Egyptian military in domestic society." *US Army. Washington, DC: Department of Defense, FMSO Report.* https://
community.apan.org/wg/tradoc-g2/fmso/m/fmso-monographs/240947.

Gretchen, Peters. 2017. *How Opium Profits the Taliban.* Washington. DC: USIP.

Gurr, Ted Robert.1970. *Why Men Rebel.* London: Routledge.

———. 1993. "Why minorities rebel: A global analysis of communal mobilization
and conflict since 1945." *International Political Science Review* 14 (2): 161–201.

Hafez, Mohamed. 2003. *Why Muslims Rebel.* London: Routledge.

Hamed, Enas. 2014. "Egyptian security forces abuse female detainees." *Al Monitor.*
February 19, 2014. https://www.al-monitor.com/originals/2014/02/egypt-female
-prisoners-abuse.html

Hammer, Joshua. 2017. "How Egypt's Activists Became 'Generation Jail.'" *The
New York Times*, March 14, 2017. https://www.nytimes.com/2017/03/14/magazine
/how-egypts-activists-became-generation-jail.html

Hamzawy, Amr. 2017. *Legislating Authoritarianism: Egypt's New Era of Repression*
16. Washington, DC: Carnegie Endowment for International Peace.

———. 2014. *Egypt 2011–15: How Can a Democratic Revolution Fail to Improve
Human Rights Conditions?* Routledge Handbook on Human Rights and the Middle
East and North Africa. https://doi/10.4324/9781315750972.ch33.

Hendawy, Abdallah. 2017. *Corruption: a lifeline for extremist groups in Libya.* In
"The Big Spin Corruption and the Growth of Violent Extremism." Lt Col Dave
Allen, GBR-A; Will Cafferky; Abdallah Hendawy; Jordache Horn; Karolina
MacLachlan; Stefanie Nijssen; Eleonore Vidal de la Blache Editor: Leah Wawro,
Karolina MacLachlan. 2017. United Kingdom: Transparency International. https://
ti-defence.org/wp-content/uploads/2017/02/The_Big_Spin_Web-1.pdf. Hoffman,
E. A. 2007. "Open-ended Interviews, Power, and Emotional Labor." *Journal of
Contemporary Ethnography* 36 (3): 318–346.

Hendawy, Abdallah. 2015. "The Dilemma of Justice in Egypt." Richmond. *The International Policy Digest* 11 (1): Art. 3.

———. 2018 "The Danger That Lurks in Sisi's Egypt." *Reuters*. https://www.reuters.com/article/us-hendawy-egypt-commentary-idUSKCN1HC2EZ.

Hochschild, Arlie R. 1983. *The Managed Heart: Commercialization of Human Feeling*. Berkeley: University of California Press.

Horgan, J. 2004. *The Psychology of Terrorism* 2. New York: Routledge.

———. 2008. "Deradicalization or Disengagement? A Process in Need of Clarity and a Counterterrorism Initiative in Need of Evaluation." *Perspectives on Terrorism* 2 (4): 3–8. Baltimore, MD: The John Hopkins University Press.

Human Rights Watch. 2014. "All According to Plan: The Rab'aa Massacre and Mass Killings of Protesters in Egypt." *Nueva York: Human Rights Watch*. August 12, 2014.

———. 2017. "Egypt: Torture Epidemic May Be Crime Against Humanity." *Human Rights Watch*. September 6, 2017.

Hunt, Scott, R. Benford, and David Snow. 1994. "Identity fields: Framing processes and social construction of movement identities." *New Social Movements: From ideology to identity*. Enrique Larana, Jank Johnston, and J. Gusfield, eds. Philadelphia: Temple University Press.

Huntington, Samuel. 1993. "Clash of Civilizations?" *Foreign Affairs* 72 (3): 22–49.

Iannaccone, Lawrence R. 1997. "Deregulating Religion: The Economics of Church and State." *Economic Inquiry* 35 (2).

Iannaccone, Lawrence R., and Eli Berman. 2006. "Religious Extremists: The Good, the Bad and the Deadly." *Public Choice* 128 (1–2): 109–129.

Ibn Hanbal, Ahmad. *English Translation of: Musnad Imam ibn Hanbal*. Al–Khattab, Nasiruddin, Trans. Al–Khattab, Huda, ed. Darussalam. (1–3): 164–241 AH, 780–855 CE.

Ibrahim, Saad Elddin. 1998. *Egypt, Islam, and democracy*. Cairo. Cairo University Press.

———. 2013. *Post-Modern Egypt and Social Change*. Translated from Arabic. Cairo: Cairo University Press.

"In Charge of the Field Hospital in Rab'a Al–Adawiya." 2013. YouTube Video, 2:30. Posted by "Aljazeera Channel." July 27, 2013. https://www.youtube.com/watch?v=7VLbX0kj3T0.

"Interview of Ramadan Khairy," 2017. YouTube video. Recorded from a TV Interview on CBC Channel. Posted by "CBC Egypt." https://www.youtube.com/watch?v=ubgdoUjgbNg.

IRIN. 2008. "Egypt: Are attitudes to rape beginning to change?" *Refworld*. February 19, 2008. https://www.refworld.org/docid/47bea83fc.html.

Jamāz, 'Alī Muḥammad, and Aḥmad ibn Muḥammad Ibn Ḥanbal. 1990. *Musnad al-Shāmīyīn min Musnad al-Imām Aḥmad ibn Ḥanbal*. Al-Dawḥah, Dawlat Qaṭar: Dār al-Thaqāfah.

Jessop, Bob. 1990. "Putting States in their Place." *State Theory: Putting Capitalist States in Their Place*. Philadelphia: Penn State University Press, 338–369.

Juergensmeyer, Mark. 2003. *Terror in the Mind of God: The Global Rise of Religious Violence*. University of California Press.

"Judge ejects defence lawyer and orders him detained for 'insulting court' at trial." 2015. YouTube video, 1:44. Recorded from Sultan Essam's video recording during court proceedings. Posted by "AP Archive." July 25, 2015. https://www.youtube.com/watch?v=_WdLK8DgUsc.

Kandil, Wael. 2012. "The Fairmont Accord Between the President and Political Parties." *Al Shorok News*. July 7, 2012. https://www.shorouknews.com/columns/view.aspx?cdate=06072012&id=a87dcc81-d96c-42f1-afe4-d2b5db538938.

Kaplan, Abraham. 1964. *The Conduct of Inquiry*. San Francisco: Chandler.

Katz, Jack. 1988. *Seductions of Crime: Moral and Sensual Attractions of Doing Evil*. New York, NY: Basic Books.

Kemper, Theodore. 2001. "A Structural Approach to Social Movement Emotions." *Passionate Politics: Emotions and Social Movements* Jeff Goodwin, James M. Jasper, Francesca Polletta, eds. University of Chicago Press.

Khamis, Sahar, and Katherine Vaughn. 2013. "Cyberactivism in the Tunisian and Egyptian Revolutions: Potentials, limitations, overlaps and divergences." *Journal of African Media Studies* 5 (1): 69–86.

Khamsi, Roxanne. 2007. "Psychological torture as bad as physical torture." *New Scientist*. USA. University Press.

Kirkpatrick, David. 2012. "Citing Deadlock, Egypt's Leader Seizes New Power and Plans Mubarak Retrial." *The New York Times*. November 22, 2012. https://www.nytimes.com/2012/11/23/world/middleeast/egypts-president-morsi-gives-himself-new-powers.html.

———. 2018. "Egypt's President Morsi Gives Himself New Powers." *The New York Times*, November 23. 2012. https://www.nytimes.com/2012/11/23/world/middleeast/egypts-president-morsi-gives-himself-new-powers.html

Koudous, Sharif Abdel. 2015. "Op-Ed: Egypt's Judiciary: A Willing Participant in Repression." *Los Angeles Times*. 2015. https://www.latimes.com/opinion/op-ed/la-oe-kouddous-egypt-20150423-story.html.

Krueger, Alan B., and Jitka Maleckova. 2002. "Education, poverty, political violence and terrorism: Is there a causal connection?" *National Bureau of Economic Research Working Paper*. July 2002. https://doi.org/10.3386/w9074.

Kuehnert, Jassmin. 2013. "Heroes, Activists, and Martyrs: Lending their names to the streets of Tehran." ACEI Global. January 24, 2013. https://acei-global.blog/2013/01/24/heroes-activists-and-martyrs-lending-their-names-to-the-streets-of-tehran/.

Kurtz, Lester R., and Lee A. Smithey, eds. 2018. *The Paradox of Repression and Nonviolent Movements*. New York: Syracuse University Press.

LaFree, Gary, and Gary Ackerman. 2009. "The empirical study of terrorism: Social and legal research." *Annual Review of Law and Social Science* 1 (5): 347–374. https://doi.org/10.1146/annurev.lawsocsci.093008.131517.

Lagon, Mark P., and Arch Puddington. 2015. "Exploiting Terrorism as a Pretext for Repression." *The Wall Street Journal* 15. January 27, 2015.

Lazare, Aaron. 1987. "Shame and humiliation in the medical encounter." *Archives of Internal Medicine* 147 (9): 1653–1658.

Le Bon, Gustav. 1916. *Psychology of Crowds.* Sparkling Books edition. Sparkling Books.

Levi, Margaret. 1997. *Consent, Dissent and Patriotism* (1): 1–525. New York: Cambridge University Press.

Lewis, Bernard. 2002. *What went wrong? Western impact and Middle Eastern response.* Oxford University Press.

Lewis, Helen B. 1971. *Shame and Guilt in Neurosis.* New York: International Universities Press, 525.

Lohr, Sabina. 2016. "The Tradition of Family Revenge Killings in Upper Egypt." Blog, Connect the Cultures. September 19, 2016. https://www.connectthecultures .com/revenge-killings-upper-egypt/.

Magouirk, Justin, Scott Atran, and Marc Sageman. 2008."Connecting terrorist networks." *Studies in Conflict & Terrorism* 31 (1): 1–16. https://doi.org /10.1080/10576100701759988.

Mahmoud, M. 2016. "Massacre in Rabaa Three years on, Egyptians reflect on the worst attack on protesters in modern history." *Aljazeera.* Cairo. August 17, 2016. https://www.aljazeera.com/programmes/aljazeeraworld/2016/08/massacre -rabaa-160816085846897.html.

Mandaville, Peter. 2001. *Transnational Muslim Politics: Reimagining the Umma* 1. London: Routledge Publishers.

———. 2005. "Sufis and Salafis: The Political Discourse of Transnational Islam." In *Remaking Muslim Politics: Pluralism, Contestation, Democratization*, Robert W. Hefner, ed. Princeton: Princeton University Press, 302–325.

———. 2014. *Islam and Politics.* London and New York: Routledge.

Maret, Susan. 2018. "Global terrorism database." *The Charleston Advisor* 19 (3): 14–19.

Mason, T. David, and Dale A. Krane. 1989. "The political economy of death squads: Toward a theory of the impact of state-sanctioned terror." *International Studies Quarterly* 33 (2): 175–198.

Matthies–Boon, Vivienne. 2017. "Shattered worlds: political trauma amongst young activists in post–revolutionary Egypt." *The Journal of North African Studies* 22 (4): 620–644.

Marcussen H., R. Gurr, J. Quiroga, and O. V. Rasmussen.. 2001. "Approaches to torture rehabilitation: a desk study covering effects, cost–effectiveness, participation, and sustainability." *Copenhagen: International Rehabilitation Council for Torture Victims* 11 (1): 1–36.

Mazoz, Abdel Ghany. 2018. "Transformations of the Jihadist Political Discourse." Istanbul, Turkey: Egyptian Studies Institute.

McAdam, Doug. 1982. *Political process and the development of black insurgency, 1930–1970.* University of Chicago Press.

McAdam, Doug, and Sidney Tarrow. 2000. "Nonviolence as Contentious Interaction." *PS: Political Science and Politics* 33 (2): 149–154.

McCarthy, John D., and Mayer N. Zald. 1977. "Resource mobilization and social movements: A partial theory." *American Journal of Sociology* 82 (6): 1212–1241.

McCauley, Clark. 2017. "Toward a Psychology of Humiliation in Asymmetric Conflict." *American Psychologist* 72: 255–265. http://psycnet.apa.org/journals/amp/72/3/255/.

McCauley, Clark and Sophia Moskalenko. 2011. *Friction: How Radicalization Happens to Them and Us*. Oxford, UK: Oxford University Press, 865–866.

McCoy, Alfred. (2007). *A Question of Torture: CIA Interrogation, from the Cold War to the War on Terror*. Henry Holt & Co., 16–17.

McCullough, Michael E., Shelley D. Kilpatrick, Robert A. Emmons, and David B. Larson. 2001. "Is gratitude a moral affect?" *Psychological Bulletin* 127 (2): 249.

McTighe, Kristen. 2015. "Squalor and death in Egypt's prisons." *Deutsche Welle News,* June 2, 2015. http://www.dw.com/en/squalor-and-death-in-egypts-prisons/a-18490546.

Mercy Corps Policy Brief. 2015. "From Jordan to Jihad: The Lure of Syria's Violent Extremist Groups." *Mercy Corps*, September 28, 2015. https://www.mercycorps.org/research-resources/jordan-jihad-syria-extremist-groups.

Mitchell, Richard P. 1969. *The Society of the Muslim Brothers*. Oxford University Press.

Mitchell, Timothy. 2002. *Rule of Experts Egypt, Techno-Politics, Modernity*. University of California Press.

Moghadam, Valentine M. 2012. *Globalization and social movements: Islamism, feminism, and the global justice movement*. Lanham, MD: Rowman & Littlefield Publishers.

Moghaddam, Fathali M. 2005. "The staircase to terrorism: A psychological exploration." *American Psychologist* 60 (2): 161–169.

Moïsi, Dominique. 2007. "The Clash of Emotions–Fear, Humiliation, Hope, and the New World Order." *Foreign Affairs* 86 (1): 8.

"Monitor Special | El-Sisi: The military spokesman is an important factor in attracting women . . . and the army's plan to control the media." 2013. YouTube video, 6:30. Posted by "Network Monitoring." October 2, 2013. https://www.youtube.com/watch?v=WB9MVTR02YE.

Montgomery, Devin. 2008. "US detainee abuses approved by senior officials: Senate report." *JURIST*, December 16, 2008.

Moore, Will H. 1998. "Repression and dissent: Substitution, context, and timing." *American Journal of Political Science* 42 (3): 851–873.

Mueller, John. 2000. "The banality of 'ethnic war'." *International Security* 25 (1): 42–70.

Muller, Edward N., and Karl-Dieter Opp. 1986. "Rational choice and rebellious collective action." *American Political Science Review* 80 (2): 471–488.

Munck, Ronaldo. 1985. "The 'Modern' Military Dictatorship in Latin America: The Case of Argentina (1976–1982)." *Latin American Perspectives* 12 (4): 41–74. https://journals.sagepub.com/doi/10.1177/0094582X8501200403.

Nadim Centre for Rehabilitation. 2006. "Torture in Egypt: A State Policy." https://www.dr.dk/NR/rdonlyres/2B705A52-EB04-4D7F-9FF8-6D91A2DA CB7C/2848081/Torture_in_Egypt_20032006.pdf.

Nagib, Muhammed. 1984. "I was the President of Egypt." *El Maktab El Masry El Hadith.*

Nameer, Ahmed. 2001. "Rape and Fear in the Arab World." Ph.D. Dissertation. Cairo University.

National Center for Social and Criminological Research Study. 2016. "On honor crimes in Egypt." *United Nations: Economic and Social Commission for Western Asia.* https://www.unescwa.org/search–results?search_api_views_fulltext=1.

Neumann, Peter. 2015. "Western European Foreign Fighters in Syria: An Overview." *Countering Violent Extremism: Developing an Evidence Base for Policy and Practice* 1: 13–19. Australia: Curtin University.

OHCHR. 2013. "Article 1.1" *United Nations Human Rights Office of the High Commissioner.* OHCHR | Convention against Torture. https://www.ohchr.org/en /professionalinterest/pages/cat.aspx.

Ohmae, Kenichi. 1996. *The End of the Nation-State: The Rise of Regional Economies.* New York: Free Press.

Ong, Aihwa. 2006. *Neoliberalism as Exception: Mutations in Citizenship and Sovereignty.* Durham, NC: Duke University Press.

Orum, Anthony M., and John G. Dale. 2008. *Political Sociology: Power and Participation in the Modern World.* New York and Oxford: Oxford University Press.

Ouaissa, Rachid, and Benoît Challand. 2014. "Has the Middle Class Been a Moto of the Arab Spring?" *Meta Journal: Topics and Arguments* 2: 12–16.

The Oxford Dictionary of Islam, 2018. "Sahih al-Bukhari." ed. John L. Esposito. *The Oxford Islamic Studies Online*, April 25, 2018. http://www.oxfordislamicstudies .com/article/opr/t125/e2056.

Papadopoulos, Dimitris, Niamh Stephenson, and Vassilis Tsianos. 2015. *Escape Routes: Control and Subversion in the Twenty-First Century.* Pluto Press.

Pape, Robert. 2005. *Dying to Win the Strategic Logic of Suicide Terrorism.* New York: Random House.

Parrenas, Rhacel. 2001. *Servants of Globalization: Women, Migration, and Domestic Work.* Stanford: Stanford University Press.

Pierterse, Jan Nederveen. 2009. *Globalization and Culture.* Lanham: Rowman & Littlefield Publishers, Inc.

Polletta, Francesca. 1999. "Snarls, Quarks, and Quarrels: Culture and Structure in Political Process Theory." *Sociological Forum* 14 (1): 63–70.

Project on the Middle East—POMED, Updated: July 2017. https://pomed.org/wp -content/uploads/2016/11/POMEDAnsaryEgyptReport.pdf.

Qazi, Shehzad H. 2011. "De–radicalizing the Pakistani Taliban." *Huffington Post* 10. http://www.huffingtonpost.com/shehzad-h-qazi/de-radicalizing-the-pakistani -taliban_b_993208.html.

Qutub, Sayyid.1988. *Milestones.* Egypt: Kazi Publications.

Ra'ef, Ahmed. 1997. *Saradeb El Shaitan.* Cairo, Egypt: Al Zahra Arab Media Production.

Rafiq, Zakaria. 2004. *Indian Muslims: where have they gone wrong?* Popular Prakashan Publishers.

Rawlins, Williams K. (1992). *Communication and social order. Friendship matters: Communication, dialectics, and the life course.* Hawthorne, NY, US: Aldine de Gruyter.

Reporters Without Borders (RSF). 2018. "Egyptian intelligence services extend control over media." *Reporters Without Borders, News.* https://rsf.org/en/news /egyptian-intelligence-services-extend-control-over-media.

Robben, Antonius. 2010. *Political violence and trauma in Argentina.* University of Pennsylvania Press.

Rudolph, Susanne Hoeber. 1997. "Introduction: Religion, states, and transnational civil society." *Transnational religion and fading states* 1: 1–24. Westview Press.

Sageman, Marc. 2004. *Understanding terror networks.* University of Pennsylvania Press. http://dx.doi.org/10 .9783/9780812206791.

Salaheldin, Ahmed A. 2015. "Conscription in Egypt: The Good, the Bad, and the Ugly." Ph.D. Dissertation. Egypt. Cairo University Archive.

Sayigh, Yezid. 2019. *Owners of the Republic: An Anatomy of Egypt's Military Economy.* Carnegie Endowment for International Peace.

Scheff, Thomas. J. 2000. *Bloody revenge: Emotions, nationalism, and war.* Boulder, CO: Westview Press.

———. 2007. "Runaway nationalism: Alienation, shame, and anger." *The self-conscious emotions: Theory and research* 1: 426–442. New York, NY: Guilford Press.

Schmid, A., and Jannie de Graaf. 1982. *Violence as Communication.* Beverly Hills, CA: Sage

Schulz, M. S., and R.S. Lazarus. (2012). "Emotion regulation during adolescence: A cognitive-mediational conceptualization." *Adolescence and beyond: Family inter-actions and transitions to adulthood* 1: 19–42. New York, NY: Oxford University Press.

Sewell, William H. 1996. "Historical Events as Transformations of Structures: Inventing Revolution at the Bastille." *Theory and Society* 25 (6): 841–881.

Shaban, Abdul Hussein. (2015). "Is it Impossible to Combat Radicalism?" *Al-Jazeera News.*

Shahzad, S. 2001. "Al Qaeda Primed for Wider Struggle." *Asia Times.* Retrieved February 14, 2001.

Shalaby, Asma. 2016. "Statistics: 92 percent of the murders of women are committed by their families because of 'honor.'" *Al-Elaan,* July 11, 2016.

Sjoberg, Gideon, ed. 1967. *Ethics, Politics, and Social research.* Cambridge, MA: Schenkman Publishing Company.

Skocpol, Theda. 1979. *States and Social Revolutions: A Comparative Analysis of France, Russia, and China.* Cambridge: Cambridge University Press.

Smelser, Neil J., and Mitchell Faith, ed. 2002. *Terrorism: Perspectives from the Behavioral and Social Sciences.* Washington, DC: The Natl. Acad. Press

Smith Brent L. 1994. *Terrorism in America: Pipe Bombs and Pipe Dreams.* Albany, New York: State University at New York Press.

Smith, Brent L., Kelly R. Damphousse, Freedom Jackson, and Amy Sellers. 2002 "The prosecution and punishment of international terrorists in federal courts: 1980–1998." *Criminology & Public Policy* 1 (3): 311–338.

Smith, Jackie. 1998. "Global Civil Society? Transnational Social Movement Organizations and Social Capital." *American Behavioral Scientist* 42 (1): 93–107.

———. 2008. *Social Movements for Global Democracy*. Baltimore, MD: The Johns Hopkins University Press.

Smith, Michael Peter. 1994. "Can you imagine? Transnational migration and the globalization of grassroots politics." *Social Text* (39): 15–33.

Snow, David A. 2004. "Framing processes, ideology, and discursive fields." *The Blackwell companion to social movements* 1: 380–412.

Snow, David A., and Robert D. Benford. 1988. "Ideology, frame resonance and movement participation." *International Social Movement Research* 1 (1): 197–217.

———. 1992. "Master frames and cycles of protest." *Frontiers in Social Movement Theory* 133: 155.

Snyder, David. 1976. "Theoretical and methodological problems in the analysis of governmental coercion and collective violence." *Journal of Political & Military Sociology* 4: 277–293.

Snyder, C. Rick, Susie C. Sympson, Florence C. Ybasco, Tyrone F. Borders, Michael A. Babyak, and Raymond L. Higgins. 1996. "Development and validation of the State Hope Scale." *Journal of Personality and Social Psychology* 70 (2): 321–325.

Somnier, Finn E., and Inge Kemp Genefke. 1986. "Psychotherapy for victims of torture." *The British Journal of Psychiatry* 149 (3): 323–329. https://doi.org/10.1192/bjp.149.3.323.

Staniland, Paul. 2014. *Networks of Rebellion: Explaining Insurgent Cohesion and Collapse*. Cornell University Press.

Statement and Position Papers. 2013. "Non-peaceful assembly does not justify collective punishment." *Cairo Institute for Human Rights Studies*. August 15, 2013. https://www.webcitation.org/6J0bTKpiI?url=http://www.cihrs.org/?p%3D7060%26lang%3Den.

"Statement of the National Revolutionary Forces Caucus." 2013. YouTube video, 4:59. Posted by "Yaqeen News Network 2." July 7, 2013. https://www.youtube.com/watch?v=dwuY4bHDuyo.

"Statement of the Sheikh of Al-Azhar d. Ahmed Al-Tayeb to the nation about the dispersal of the sit-in Rab'aa Al-Adawiya and Al-Nahda." YouTube video, 2:31. Voice in a televised statement. Posted by "24.ae." August 14, 2013. https://www.youtube.com/watch?v=sKEAxbZKLug.

Sterling, Claire. 1981. *The Terror Network: The Secret War of International Terrorism*. Weidenfeld and Nicolson.

Stern, Jessica. 2003. *Terror in the Name of God: Why Religious Militants Kill*. New York: Ecco.

Supreme Council of Armed Forces SCAF Statement. 2013. "Egypt military unveils transitional roadmap." *Ahram Online*. 3 July 2013. https://english.ahram.org.eg/News/75631.aspx.

Tammam, Hussam. 2013. *The Muslim Brotherhood: The Year the Preceded the Revolution*. El Shorouk Print.

Tangney, June. 2014. "After committing a crime, guilt and shame predict re-offense." *Association for Psychological Science*. February 11, 2014. https://www.psycholog icalscience.org/news/releases/after-committing-a-crime-guilt-and-shame-predict -re-offense.html.

Tarabay, Chanelle, and Wayne Warburton. 2017. "Anger, aggression and violence: It matters that we know the difference." *The Conversation*. September 1, 2017. https://theconversation.com/anger-aggression-and-violence-it-matters-that-we -know-the-difference-82918.

Tarrow, Sidney. 1994. *Power in Movement: Social Movements, Collective Actions, and Politics*. Cambridge University Press.

———. 2005. *The New Transnational Activism*. New York: Oxford University Press.

"Tehran Municipality." 2021. Tehran: The Official Website of Tehran Municipality. https://en.tehran.ir/.

"The testimony of Rasha Abdul Rahman for virginity tests in the military prison." 2012. YouTube video, 7:32. Posted by "Egyptian Initiative for Personal Rights— EIPR." February 25, 2012. https://www.youtube.com/watch?v=heemiSNW94k.

Tillmann–Healy, L. 2003. "Friendship as Method." *Qualitative Inquiry* 9 (5): 729–749.

Tilly, Charles. 1989. "Cities and States in Europe, 1000–1800." *Theory and Society* 18: 563–584.

Tilly, Charles. 1978. *From Mobilization to Revolution*. McGraw-Hill.

Tilley, Helen. 2011. *Africa as a Living Laboratory: Empire, Development, and the Problem of Scientific Knowledge, 1870–1950*. University of Chicago Press.

TIMEP. 2014. "Ajnad Misr." *The Tahrir Institute for Middle East Policy*, July 22, 2014. https://timep.org/esw/non-state-actors/ajnad-misr/

———. 2017. "Security Watch." *The Tahrir Institute for Middle East Policy*. https:// timep.org/analysis/security-terrorism/

Tocqueville, Alexis de. 1955. *The Old Régime and the French Revolution*. Paris: Anchor Books.

Tong, Eddie M.W., Barbara L. Fredrickson, Weining Chang, and Zi Xing Lim. 2010. "Re-examining hope: The roles of agency thinking and pathways thinking." *Cognition and Emotion* 24 (7): 1207–1215.

Turk, Austin T. 1982. *Political Criminality: The Defiance and Defense of Authority*. Beverly Hills, CA: Sage.

———. 2002a. "Assassination." *Encyclopedia of Crime and Justice* 2 (1): 776–81. New York: Macmillan.

———. 2002b. "Policing international terrorism: options." *Police Pact. Res.* 3 (4): 279–286.

———. 2002c. "Terrorism." *Encyclopedia of Crime and Justice*, J. Dressler, ed. 2 (4): 1549–1556. New York: Macmillan.

———. 2004. "Sociology of Terrorism." *Annual Review of Sociology* 30 (1): 271–286.

"Uniquely. . . the Brotherhood is taking advantage of the poor to support their demonstrations." 2014. YouTube video, 6:24. A video report on Muslim Brotherhood exploitation and violence. Posted by "Dream TV Egypt." April 14, 2014. https://www.youtube.com/watch?v=B5GGpG0EeOU.

"US Army Training and Doctrine Command TRADOC G2." 2007. *A Military Guide to Terrorism in the Twenty-First Century*. Fort Leavenworth, KS: TRADOC Intelligence Support Activity-Threats. https://fas.org/irp/threat/terrorism/guide.pdf.

Van Doorn, Janne, Marcel Zeelenberg, and Seger M. Breugelmans. 2014. "Anger and prosocial behavior." *Emotion Review* 6 (3): 261–268. https://doi.org/10.1177/1754073914523794.

Van Doorn, Janne. 2018. "Anger, feelings of revenge, and hate." *Emotion Review* 10 (4): 321–322.

Victoroff, Jeff. 2005. "The mind of the terrorist: A review and critique of psychological approaches." *Journal of Conflict Resolution* 49 (1): 3–42.

Von Behr, Ines, Anais Reding, Charlie Edwards, and Luke Gribbon. 2013. *Radicalisation in the Digital Era: The Use of the Internet in 15 Cases of Terrorism and Extremism*. Brussels: Rand, Europe. RAND Corporation.

Waller, James E. 2006. *Becoming evil: How ordinary people commit genocide and mass killing*. Oxford University Press.

Walton, John. 1984. *Reluctant Rebels: Comparative Studies of Revolution and Underdevelopment*. New York: Columbia University Press.

———. 1991. *Western Times and Water Wars: State, Culture, and Rebellion in California*. University of California Press.

"Weapons seized during the dispersal of the Rab'aa and al-Nahda sit-ins." 2013. YouTube Video, 1:43, August 14, 2013. Posted by "Al Watan News." https://www.youtube.com/watch?v=owIS8IqiRek.

Weber, Ingmar, Rama Venkata, Garimella Kiran, and Batayneh Alaa. 2013. "Secular vs. Islamist polarization in Egypt on Twitter." *IEEE/ACM International Conference on Advances in Social Networks Analysis and Mining* (ASONAM 2013).

Wedeman, Ben, Reza Sayah, and Matt Smith. 2013. "Coup topples Egypt's Morsy; deposed president under 'house arrest.'" *CNN News*. July 4, 2013.

Wiktorowicz, Quintan. 2004. "Joining the cause: Al-Muhajiroun and radical Islam." *The Roots of Radical Islam*. Syracuse, New York: Institute for Security Policy and Law.

———. 2005. *Radical Islam rising: Muslim extremism in the West*. Rowman & Littlefield Publishers.

Yousef, Ahmed, and Mohamed El Bahrawy. 2014. "El Farafra Attack." *Al Masry Al Youm Newspaper*. September 20, 2014. https://www.almasryalyoum.com/news/details/486352.

Zidan, Youssef. 2009. *Arab Theology and the Origins of Religious Violence*. Cairo, Egypt: Al Shourok Press.

Index

About the Author

Abdallah Hendawy specializes in the study of mass mobilization and social movements with a particular focus on radicalization and violent insurgency in the Middle East. He has been actively engaged in several grassroots organizations and managed transnational action movements. Hendawy continues to provide analyses of regional developments for several think tanks, international organizations, and other global platforms. Hendawy holds a Ph.D. in Sociology from George Mason University.

www.ingramcontent.com/pod-product-compliance
Lightning Source LLC
Chambersburg PA
CBHW050614280326
41932CB00016B/3044